r·Gropius

Wassily·Kandinsky

Paul·Klee

BAUHAUS

1933

GEOMETRY NOW!

DESIGNING FOR TOMORROW

sendp●ints

Designing for Tomorrow

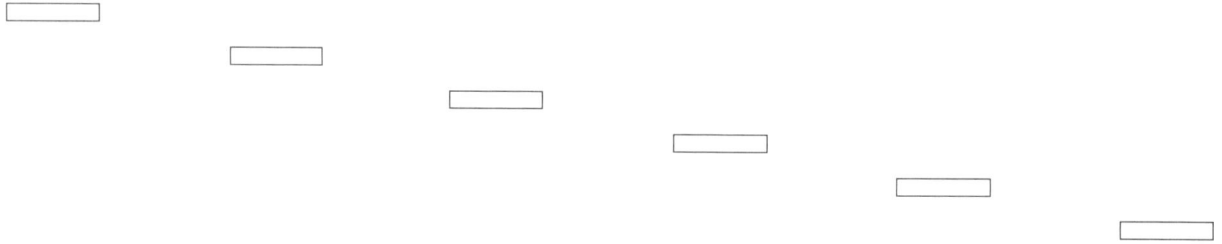

As the indispensable visual element in graphic design, geometric shapes are chased after among graphic designers and have been given credit for numerous classic designs featuring the ingenious use of these shapes. Geometry, the science that studies shapes, takes visual thinking as the leading role and is dedicated to improving human outsight and spatial imagination. Geometric shapes stand at the core of geometry and boast preciseness and accuracy in the framework of mathematical principles. Therefore, the inclusion of geometric shapes would make the designs rather accurate and concise, attracting people with the beauty of the structure.

Euclid, the "Father of Geometry", developed geometry into a discipline with a rigorous theoretical system and scientific methods as far back as 3 000 B.C., and gradually made mathematics a fancy topic for common people. The combination of figures and geometry brought forth magical sparkles that have been fascinating people for over two millennia.

Reason dominated the early Western civilization. Imitation and objective realism had been the mainstream of European art until the Renaissance. It was at the turn of 19th century that the geometric shapes made a figure in Western art. The rapid development of industrialization and the social unrest ushered in the era with the most active thinking when modern art enjoyed unprecedented prosperity, and various schools and thoughts kept coming out. The artists made bold experiments to surpass or reject traditional realism both in the artistic ideology and in the technique of expression, exerting enormous impacts on modern design. For example, some schools of art took the initiative to incorporate geometric shapes in artistic creation, which has made a far-reaching influence on modern art and inspired artists to creatively apply geometry in artistic design.

When it came to the beginning of the 20th century, Cubism emerged as the most influential movement of modern art pioneered by Pablo Picasso and Georges Braque. The artists attempted to break loose from the perception and introduced the reason in the graphic design, putting an end to the blind adoration of such laws of nature as the areal perspective in traditional painting. Hence, geometric elements and shapes became pervasive in the artistic creation.

De Stijl made a great breakthrough in the application of geometry in graphic art. The artists who pursued pure abstraction and simple style and advocated to depict images with geometric forms of mechanical beauty in the most concise and clearest manner, arranged painting layout and proportion following rigorous mathematical calculations. The visual language, as a result, tended to be characterized by high rationalization, functionalization, minimalism, and geometric formalization.

The Russian Constructivism bore favorable artistic comparison with the above art schools. The constructivists explored new forms of expression in graphic design, pioneered the synthesis of geometric abstraction with photography, and created semi-abstract or abstract images composed with such geometric elements as squares, circles, and lines.

In 1919, the Bauhaus ushered in a new era of modern design with a pioneering and enterprising spirit, exerting a strong influence on the style of modernism. It advocated that all artists turn to practical art and separate design from art. The artists analyzed forms with simple geometric elements and dedicated themselves to simplify the form, pursuing a simple, functionalized, and accurate graphic design characterized with geometrization and high rationalization step by step. The frequent application of geometric elements in commercial designs contributed to the popularity of geometry among the common public, and gradually made this technique of expression a classic in graphic design.

The geometric elements in graphic design flourished under the advocacy of the Bauhaus and kept going on even after the Bauhaus was forced to close down in 1933. Influenced by Bauhaus and other artistic styles, Swedish Internationalism had spread throughout the major powers after World War II. The modern graphic design in the United States and Japan enjoyed a strong momentum of development as well. In the new-round development of graphic design, geometric shapes remained a dominant position, constantly innovating new visual language.

Geometric elements never fail to withstand the test of time. "Less is More", a famous aphorism put forward by Ludwig Mies van der Rohe over 100 years ago, is still cited by designers in various fields who admire the classic and timeless minimalism style advocated by the master. A century ago when the vitality of art was unleashed, geometry shapes, which were popular among all art genres, constantly inspired designers to deliver thousands of masterpieces. Now, with the precious legacy left by the master, we should keep on exploring the application of geometry shapes in graphic design. Let's design for tomorrow.

1907 Cubism
P.006

1915 Constructivism
P.016

1917 De Stijl
P.026

1907 Cubism

CUBISM

In 1907, Cubism made a stage pose in France. As an important revolution in modern art, it profoundly changed the stereotypical methods of traditional painting, i.e., depicting the three-dimensional space in the use of one-point perspective, posing a challenge to the traditional aesthetic in the styles of structural distortion and absurd incongruity. It was the first time that the geometrical elements showed extraordinary brilliance in the artistic creation including painting and sculpture. As for this bold breakthrough in arts, some artists resisted and regarded it as a deviation from the long-lasting painting tradition in Europe since Renaissance, while others got fascinated by the novel and charming expression.

Paul Cézanne, the Enlightener of Cubism

Although Pablo Picasso (Spain) and Georges Braque (France) are universally accepted as key founders of Cubism, it has proved that the movement dates back to around 1900 when Paul Cézanne, a French impressionist, was exploring the "truth" in painting. Unlike other impressionist masterpieces, Cézanne's paintings give special attention to the structure. He decomposed objects of all forms into elements and then reconstituted them into geometric shapes with the beauty of simplicity in his artistic creation.

Cézanne once said, "treat nature by the cylinder, the sphere, the cone." The nature depicted in his works features a simple style and geometric charm.

It is clear to see that Paul Cézanne's artistic expression in the later works is a far cry from his early period of creation, which is particularly noticeable in *The Card Players* and *Woman with a Coffee Pot* featuring geometric patterns almost everywhere. He turned to the abstract geometric expressions to depict a figure with cylindrical arms and sphere head — almost all body parts and facial features were presented in basic geometric shapes. In these figure paintings, most details including background light were depicted with rectangles, triangles, trapezoids, and such. In addition to figure paintings, geometry is spotted in his carefully crafted still life paintings as well. In his representative work *Still Life with Basket* created from 1888 to 1890, the harmonious and varied color combinations with the geometric composition are visually striking. Among these carefully organized still life paintings, Cézanne focused on the use of geometry and colors instead of the laws of scientific perspective, space and volume.

Instead of following any set formula, his geometric configuration was conceived with careful analysis and synthesis of the natural world and each object was depicted stroke by stroke, constituting these important research steps. In his views, objectivity and accuracy should take second place to form and structure. He incorporated geometric elements into his paintings as often as he could, breaking away from the restrictions imposed by the fixed-point perspective and representation rules in the traditional Western art, and thus was hailed as the "Father of Modern Painting". Moreover, the simple, delicate geometric elements that later make a conspicuous figure and take an indispensable role in artistic creation have been largely attributed to his ingenious exploration.

Proto-Cubism

The proto-Cubism is also regarded as the Cubism in the "Cézanne period", which is the first stage of Cubism. As the name implies, the then artists, under the influence of Cézanne, pursued simple geometric figures instead of lighting and color analysis.

Cubist painting began in 1907 with Picasso's *The Young Ladies of Avignon* when he was only 25 years old. It was no easy matter for the young artist to discard traditional artistic expression. To get liberated from such long-cherished western painting laws as aerial perspective, Picasso turned to Cézanne's pictorial philosophy for inspiration. The gifted young man not only got an insight into Cézanne's geometry expression but also further developed the techniques by initiating a semi-abstract form of creation to break free from the strictures of reality.

The figures and facial features of the five girls in *The Young Ladies of Avignon* are depicted in fragmented geometric shapes with a multitude of colored facets on a flat plane. The olive-shaped eyes, triangle noses, and rhombic torsos, together with the background of geometric shapes varying in size and form, highlight the geometrical elements, further drifting away from reality and tradition. Picasso threw out the spatial relations in classical art and chiaroscuro with a single light source, and built up the structure of the painting by use of multi-point perspective, color contrast, geometric combination, as well as a shadow effect. This avant-garde and grotesque expression brought a brand new visual impact.

Impressed with this expression in 1907 when Braque saw *The Young Ladies of Avignon* for the first time, he created *Large Nude* as a response, or rather as a token of accepting the challenge posed by Picasso. Braque's struggle to adopt this style in this painting was proven to be crucial to his future career. He learned to depict the nude in geometric shapes and displayed the picture structure by color contrast, departing from the traditional aesthetics. In 1908, French art critic Louis Vauxcelles spoke of him as "bold" to "reduce all images in his paintings to geometric shapes and cubes". Cubism, thus, got its name.

In the following two years from 1908 to 1909, Braque was in his study laboring away over how to generalize and shape complex objects in simple geometric forms. Influenced by Cézanne, Braque and Picasso further explored the possibilities of integrating geometry into painting with the use of multi-point perspective. Braque created *Houses at l'Estaque*, with more striking geometric elements than those in *Large Nude*, and Picasso created *Three Women, The Reservoir, Horta de Ebro* and *Woman with Pears*, gradually living up to Cézanne's instruction to "treat nature by the cylinder, the sphere, the cone". Although they were eager to make a breakthrough, the requirement of the expression for observing, generalizing and summarizing the objects prevented them from free creation, which was just like dancing with shackles. The incorporation of geometric shapes into paintings was initiated by Cézanne, but Cubists gave it a special meaning.

1907-1914
CUBISM

PAUL
CÉZANNE

Analytical Cubism

Cubism was heading to the analytical path with the persistent exploration of Picasso and Braque, and the geometric elements gained more grace in painting creation. In early 1909, Braque finished the painting *Violin and Pitcher*, which was regarded as a key breakthrough in the perception of structure in modern painting. Braque decomposed objects into geometric shapes varying in size and form, and reconstructed the fragmented parts into a geometric whole with no obvious contours. Geometry has become an indispensable part of the composition of painting rather than a trace in the process. The light and the interlaced images were used based on the structure of the painting and no longer subject to objective reality.

In 1910, Picasso expanded Cubism in his painting series *Portrait of Ambroise Vollard*, *Portrait of Wilhelm Uhde*, and *Portrait of Daniel-Henry Kahnweiler*, in which the geometric shapes remained the main elements of the structure. He fragmented the models in the paintings into geometrical elements including square, triangle, rhombic, trapezoid, circle, and irregular geometry, and then juxtaposed and overlapped these fragments. Picasso exerted himself to reconstruct the images out of his understanding and set himself free from the outline, light, and shadow of reality.

Picasso and Braque had made significant progress in Cubism from 1910 to 1912, and formed a mature style. Consequently, a series of works sprang up, including Picasso's *Man with a Pipe* and *My Beautiful*, and Braque's *Woman with a Guitar* and *Portuguese*, marking the flourishing period of Analytical Cubism. The most distinct feature of this era, compared with the previous stage, lies in the artists' focus on the internal structure. The artistic creation by decomposing and restructuring objects into a combination of geometric shapes gave rise to a new aesthetic value and liberated the form of painting unprecedentedly. The use of simple geometric shapes was given new meaning. Although Analytical Cubism appeared absurd and unreasonable from the traditional view, it greatly promoted the development of Western visual art, enlightened many young artists, and made Cubism a large-scale movement involving dozens of artists.

Synthetic Cubism

Synthetic Cubism, a more subjective, abstract, and complicated Cubism, came into being in 1912 since Picasso and Braque cannot completely part with realism. In order to resolve the contradiction between abstraction and reality, they made a new attempt at collage. They combined and modeled a variety of materials, including the old newspapers and fragments of posters in the paintings to reflect and depict the real world and achieve a harmonious artistic effect. A new graphic visual language was created, with the traditional, realistic, and concrete images replaced by the abstract geometric shapes that were represented by pieces of fragmented materials.

This new expression originated from the perceptual cognition of the world. Picasso's *Still Life with Caned Chair* in 1912 is recognized as the first collage in the history of art, with the cane-pattern canvas and "a canvas frame" made of hemp rope, blurring the line between reality and abstraction. In the painting, the lemon slices, cup, pipe, newspaper, and such objects were fragmented into abstract geometric shapes, and were incorporated into an oval composition together with the canvas, to present the image of the tabletop.

Synthetic Cubism extended geometrical elements from painting to collage, which contributed to the further breakthroughs of geometry in the visual arts. *Fruit Dish and Glass* is Braque's first collage. But in fact, his work *Homage to J.S. Bach* created as early as December 1911 already showed a tendency to the Synthetic Cubism. Although there were no collage elements in the painting, Braque depicted wood texture with a painting brush, bringing the abstract painting back to reality. In *Fruit Dish and Glass*, Braque cut off three pieces of wallpaper and put the geometric collage together with the fragmented geometric grapes, glass, and fruit tray on a plane in a harmonious manner. Afterward, they had been making unceasing exploration to make Synthetic Cubism mature little by little, with amazing creations including Picasso's *Violin, Portrait of a Young Girl* and *Bottle of Black Rum*, as well as Braque's *The Clarinet, Violin and Sheet Music on a Table* and *Glass Carafe and Newspapers*.

The Influence of Cubism

In addition to Picasso and Braque, the two founders of Cubism, other outstanding artists, who either drew inspiration from Cézanne or adored the art form itself, were also pushing the boundaries of artistic creation in Cubism.

Juan Gris is the cream of the crop in the movement, preceded only by the two founders. Enlightened by Cézanne's style, especially the clear and concise geometry, Gris gave a full expression of diagonal lines in his early paintings, to invigorate the geometric composition. Taking his masterpiece *The Watch* as an example, Gris divided the picture with vertical and horizontal lines into rectangles, and further into triangles with diagonal lines, presenting a bright, lively and harmonious composition. With a strong interest in geometry, he was quite confident in his mastery of geometric elements, claiming that all works can be simplified into pure geometry by himself. His works feature strictly accurate geometrical composition and rational expression, including *Portrait of Pablo Picasso*, *Violin and Guitar*, and *Fruit Bowl with Bottle*.

Fernand Léger was also a major figure of cubists, keen to create geometric patterns of objects instead of making geometric division and restructuring. He attempted to free his paintings from the traditional fixed-point perspective by reducing three-dimensional space into two-dimensional plane in a geometric way. In contrast with other artists, Léger was more faithful to Cézanne's emphasis on geometry to "treat nature by the cylinder, the sphere, the cone". However, due to his experiences in the World War I, he gave up the style of abstraction that other Cubist painters were pursuing, and turned to depict real life. *Geometric Standards*, *Contrast of Forms*, *Chimneys on Rooftops* and *Nudes in the Forest* are among his representative works created in the movement of Cubism.

As time passed and society changed, the pioneering and progressive spirit in Cubism faded away. The art movement gradually lost its vitality and ended abruptly with the outbreak of the World War I in 1914. Cubism has inspired modern graphic design in terms of graphic modeling and space design, as well as the use of new materials, and has exerted great influence on the United States and most European countries including Italy, Germany, and Russia.

Geometric shapes yielded unusually brilliant results in the paintings of Cubism and enjoyed unprecedented evolution in visual arts, from the geometric elements, geometric structures, to collage with geometrical composition. Such exploration was further advanced in the movements of De Stijl in Dutch and Constructivism in Russia, and especially in the Bauhaus in Germany.

1915 Constructivism

CONSTRUCTIVISM

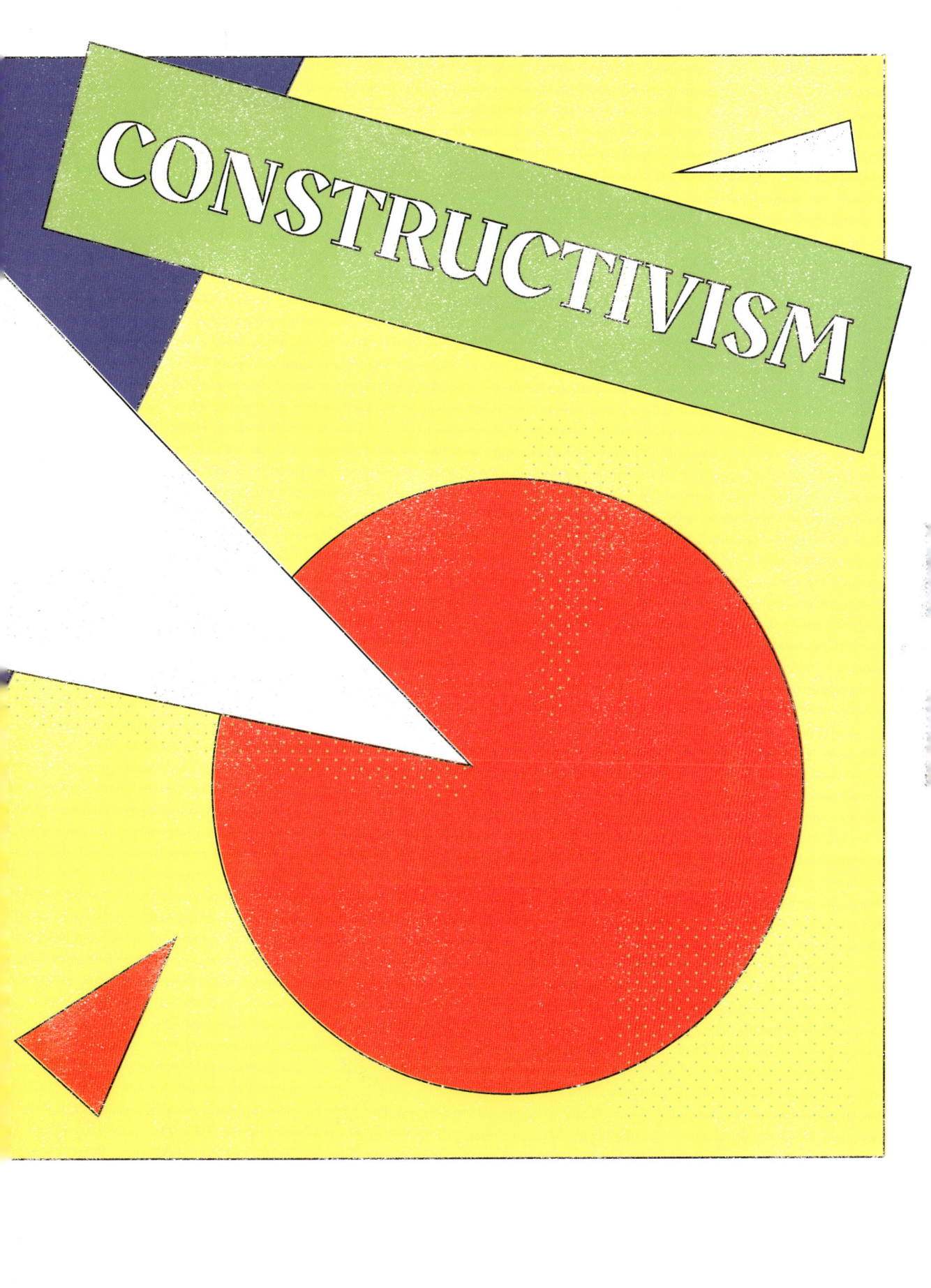

Constructivism is an avant-garde art movement and design movement emerging in Russia before the October Revolution arousing revolutionary enthusiasm nationwide. Under the background of the era, a large number of artists and designers devoted themselves to artistic creation filled with passion. Constructivism, which highlighted cultural revolution and progressive concepts, had the chance to fulfill its potential in the fields of art, architecture, and design.

Quite a lot of avant-garde artists in Russia tried to explore the practicability of the objects with techniques of abstract expression, and creatively applied the geometric shapes to graphic design. They proposed to integrate technology into art and focus on design, thus establishing a new form of art and design, namely, Constructivism. They were inclined to replace the traditional style in the czarist period with the new form and support the Revolution.

Others emphasized the spiritual world and inner experience, rejecting the traditional arts and showing the revolutionary spirit against the tradition. They advocated the primacy of abstract emotions, went away with a representational expression of traditional art, and created paintings with only abstract geometry, developing the style of Suprematism.

Graphic design and film, especially the former, were the key mass media at that time, both of which burst with great vitality in the movement of Constructivism. The pioneering work of these artists has left its own marks on the history of art and design in Russia.

Constructivism has made a great breakthrough in the expression of graphic design. Influenced by Cubism, artists introduced abstract geometric shapes in graphic design and insisted on using rectangles, circles, straight lines, and such to create a semi-abstract or abstract picture. However, unlike Cubism, Constructivism was completely divorced from the elements in reality. The artists advocated using geometry, lines, and colors in the composition, and gave the seemingly simplified combination of geometric shapes a new meaning, which helps to revitalize these designs.

There are two main forms of integrating geometric shapes into the graphic design of Constructivism: one is to use geometric shapes for dividing the paintings into segments without any special connotation, or only for decoration; the other is to give the geometric shapes meanings and use the combination of these geometric figures to express what the creators intend to convey. The latter is what El Lissitzky followed in his works.

Constructivism artists broke free from tradition and adopted the disorganized layout of Futurism for expression, building visual language with a large number of geometric combinations.

In addition, Russian constructivists creatively integrated photographic composition and font design into graphic design. In the look-ahead exploration of the use of fonts, designers emphasized the expression of fonts and proposed to use sans serif and took the extra-bold one as the main font to underline the strength of words and facilitate recognition by the public.

Although the exploration of integrating Constructivism into the architectural and industrial designs had lasted until the 1930s, it proved to be futile efforts at last. Most of the artists involved in the movement, especially those believing in Suprematism, were criticized by the public and purged. As a result, some left Russia, while most others were forced to change profession and even driven to the last-ditch due to the lack of professional and social support, or were sent to the concentration camps in Siberia.

But the new form initiated by these artists to serve the modern society and the people, especially in architectural design and graphic design, had a great impact on the formation and development of modern design style in countries worldwide, laying a solid foundation for modernist design.

Malevich, the Follower of Pure Geometry

Kazimir Severinovich Malevich, a key representative of Russian Constructivism, is acclaimed as the first abstract painter to create pure geometric shapes in the history of modern painting. His pioneering works had a profound influence on the development of abstract art in the 20th century.

In the early period, Malevich's works varied in style but under the influence of Impressionism, Fauvism, and Cubism, gradually showed a tendency of simplification mainly with pure geometric shapes and their links.

Malevich started his art creation as early as before the October Revolution. He explored and gradually formed his own constructivist style in art and design. He pursued what he named "Supremacism" by using simple geometric structures with combinations of bright and pure colors. This abstract, themeless art form was free from both the real and the imagined so as to get "the supremacy of pure feeling". He opposed pragmatism and realism in artistic creation and believed that the feeling of the artist should be expressed in an abstract and supreme way.

Black Square, created by Malevich in 1915, is an abstract geometric painting featuring extreme simplicity. He drew a square with a ruler on a piece of white canvas and then evenly painted it black, which was "an uncrossable line that demarcated the chasm between old art and new art". It made a stir in 1915 the moment it was shown in *0,10: the Last Futurist Exhibition* in Petrograd. Audiences exclaimed in front of the painting that all they adored had gone, and there was nothing in front of them except a black square on a white background.

Malevich held that art had been fragmented and interwoven with many non-artistic factors, which prevented it from being in pure forms. He was determined to renovate to free painting from superfluous and irrelevant impurities, which started from seeking for the simplest element, namely the geometric elements with *Black Square* as the most typical example, for the simple black square implied strong emotions he hid in the painting. Afterward, he had been further exploring supremacist paintings and gradually clarified the style in his works, making full use of simple geometric shapes, including circles, squares, and triangles matched with bright color pallets.

Malevich boasted another masterpiece *White on White*, in which he depicted a white square on a white canvas. He dealt with the two squares, i.e., the canvas and the square he painted, in two different ways. The painting seemed nothing special at first glance, due to the lack of colors and depth, but this was the style of Supremacism admired by Malevich. He refused to use common art techniques to create so-called "unique" paintings but insisted on creating with the purest geometric shapes. The minimalist style in *White on White* made the viewers feel rather calm and relaxed.

El Lissitzky, the Pioneer of Graphic Design

It is El Lissitzky and Alexander Rodchenko among the Russian artists of Constructivism that contributed most to graphic design. As one of the key founders of modern graphic design, El Lissitzky creatively used the geometric elements, and placed them in a rather important position, exerting a profound influence on graphic design.

Lissitzky's design showed distinct characteristics of Constructivism, namely, simple and clear style with concise vertical and horizontal composition, sans serif, and simple geometric shapes for decoration. As a designer, he refused to decorate his works but tended to adjust and design the structure to highlight the theme.

He preferred geometric elements with powerful contrast, including triangles and circles, and was adept at using diagonal compositions to keep the picture balanced and vibrant. The colors he used were varying from soft to bold.

However, different from Supremacist, Lissitzky was keen on perspective and three-dimensional presentation. He named his series of abstract paintings PROUNS, which he created with abstract and complex geometric forms, including a variety of lines, reticulation, and geometric shapes, to build a spatial structure with a three-dimensional effect on a two-dimensional plane. PROUNS is a Russian abbreviation meaning "for new art", and Lissitzky interpreted it as "an intermediary between painting and architecture".

Meanwhile, he created his most successful work *Beat the Whites with the Red Wedge*. The poster was designed with pure geometric shapes to express the profound implication the artist intended to convey: the red triangle symbolized the Bolshevik revolutionary forces; the insertion of the triangle into the white circle, a symbol of reactionary forces, made a very strong visual impact to imply the unstoppable power of the revolution. In addition, the asymmetric diagonal layout exerted a great impact on the viewers as well.

The book design would also be regarded as Lissitzky's representative graphic art besides painting and poster design, in which he followed the consistent design style and skillfully used simple geometric shapes to express his ideas. In 1923, he was responsible for the visual design of Vladimir Mayakovsky's collection of poems, *For the Voice*. The cover featured his style of composition: vertical and horizontal layout, sans serifs, and simple geometric (circular) decoration. Each poem in the collection was accompanied by a similar abstract design, mainly in red, white, and black. Furthermore, he worked with Hans Arp, a Dadaism artist, to design and publish *The Isms of Art*, building up the basis to modern layout.

These practices of Constructivism made him rank among the key founders of modern graphic design. During his stay in Germany, he introduced Russian Constructivism and Suprematism to the West by making a large number of graphic designs which received an overwhelming response in Germany and Western Europe. He also had lectures at the Bauhaus several times carrying journals and publications of Russian Constructivism, which had some effects on the development of the Bauhaus. Inspired by him, the new generation of designers was making rapid progress, culminating in the formation of modernistic and internationalist graphic design.

Geometry Now !

Alexander Rodchenko, the Co-founder of Graphic Design

Alexander Rodchenko is another graphic designer who takes a decisive position in Russian Constructivism. He made avant-garde explorations and experiments in graphic design. He was skillful in building vibrant and changing geometric space in the use of points, lines, and planes to create consistent pictures full of expressiveness, laying the foundation for graphic design.

Rodchenko was deeply influenced by Cubism and Suprematism as Lissitzky was, preferring to use simple geometric elements. Rodchenko had been engaged in fine arts creation in his early days until 1912 when Constructivism pointed out that art served the rich and powerful while the design was for the people, and that artists should turn to design. Rodchenko gave up painting and was devoted to design thenceforth, creating works featuring distinct characteristics of Constructivism.

Rodchenko began designing magazines in 1923, including the magazine *Novyi Lef*. In addition to the distinct style of Constructivism, he preferred bold typefaces, geometric shapes and lines, as well as contrasting black and white color pallets, so his works were powerful and especially eye-striking. In 1924, such techniques of expression were used in his design of Jim Dollar's series *Miss Mend*, which featured bold combinations of geometric shapes, contrasting color pallets, and collages used in cover design.

Commissioned by Dobrolyot, an early Soviet Union air transport organization, Rodchenko designed the organization's logo and a series of posters with a distinct style of Constructivism. The logo was put in a concentric circle with a diagonal line where geometrically-shaped airplane propellers lay, breaking the conventional symmetric layout.

In 1925, he designed a geometric poster for the Russian Exhibition Hall in the International Exhibition of Modern Decorative and Industrial Arts. The poster featured an asymmetric diagonal layout with letters on the diagonal line, while the square scattered on the other side of the diagonal line. The combination of letters and geometric elements, matched with a color pallet of red, white and black, and such a bold layout design drew so much attention from around the world.

1917

1917 De Stijl

DE STIJL

De Stijl has a profound influence on modernist design, like Russian Constructivism. Launched by the painter and designer Theo van Doesburg and being popular from 1917 to 1928, De Stijl was a cooperative project, an undertaking, or a loosely organized art group of young artists centering around the magazine *De Stijl* which gathered together artists and architects together to establish the aesthetics and expression for the movement. Apart from the founder Theo van Doesburg, De Stijl boasted of painters Piet Mondrian, Bart van der Leck, and such. The artists were creating in an abstract geometric style to pursue a balanced and harmonious formal language.

Mondrian preferred to use the term Neoplasticism, which was another name for De Stijl. He believed that the new idea would get rid of external details and would bring new abstract expression in forms and colors. With these restrictions, he only used vertical and horizontal geometric structures, such geometric shapes as squares and rectangles, and the colors were limited to black, white, and three primary colors.

The De Stijl artists believed that the laws of nature lived only with "absolute" abstract language. In terms of design, they advocated to use the concisely pure and abstract geometric language rather than the representational elements and concrete details, for the abstract geometric paintings, sculptures, furniture design, interior design, and architectural design had the power to convey the information in a more pure and direct manner. These attempts were put into practice by using the simple composition of horizontal and vertical lines that had "universal significance", and pure black, white, and three primary colors, pretty much the same as the techniques of expression in *De Stijl* that features vertical and horizontal layout, sans serifs, and decoration of black and white squares.

As the mainstay of the movement, Mondrian influenced the design philosophy and expression of De Stijl to a large extent, guiding the artists involved in the movement to take the style of rationalism. They erased the traces of the visual ornaments and the curve composition, and only the black vertical and horizontal lines and such geometric elements as squares and rectangles were left. Doesburg, another key figure of De Stijl, applied the theory to graphic design. He took advantage of the vertical and horizontal structure in book design, creating a quite appealing visual effect.

Bart van der Leck's paintings may have nothing to do with absolute abstract, but the "counter-composition" of the shapes is out of the nature. He preferred geometric elements including squares and rhombi, so his works presented a dynamic balance brought by the vertical and horizontal elements, in the style with a high degree of formalization and geometrization.

De Stijl stopped publication in 1928. The movement ended in 1933 for various reasons including Doesburg's death in 1931 and the political situation of Nazi Germany. However, the legacy of De Stijl has been inspiring numerous designers and architects, exerting long-lasting influence on modern art and design.

The abstract geometric expression gained great development in the De Stijl movement. Not only did the geometric figures become prominent in the paintings, but also did the concise geometric composition acquire a dominant position in the graphic design. The pure and abstract geometric visual language extracted from the strict mathematical logic, and the minimalist layout composed of repeatedly-used vertical and horizontal lines and primary colors, all have been deemed as the everlasting classic. The movement served as a key artistic form and theoretical source for modernism, and its aesthetic concept had an inestimable influence on the Bauhaus.

Theo van Doesburg, the Spiritual Leader of De Stijl

Theo van Doesburg, a painter and a designer who had started painting before the movement began, was acclaimed as the spiritual leader of the De Stijl. After exploring the traditional art of Dutch on and off, in Amsterdam in 1912, he turned to write exhibition reviews and articles on topics including Futurism, Cubism, and Kandinsky, in an attempt to establish an all-encompassing theory of modern art.

Inspired by Mondrian's art exhibition at the end of 1915, Doesburg got in touch with Mondrian in no time and consulted about starting a magazine that would further the development of modern art, namely *De Stijl*, which was finally to be published in 1917.

The creative methods and concepts Doesburg used in his early paintings were originated from the stained glass design or other applied arts, in which he pioneered the use of the rectangular element similar to the geometric ones in the paintings of Mondrian and Leck. He also used such means as rotation or inversion to create variations with simple geometries and color blocks.

Doesburg had only few correspondence with Mondrian from 1916 to 1917 and in fact, he was not at all enlightened by Mondrian on the "purely abstract art". It was Kandinsky that played a key role in leading him to the path of pursuing abstract geometry. Influenced by Kandinsky's art and theory, Doesburg tried to integrate abstract geometrical elements in his artistic creation, which can be reflected in his *Girl with Buttercups*. He pursued the "compromise in absolute freedom" proposed by Kandinsky in *Concerning the Spiritual in Art*, swaying between the two extremes of realism and purely geometric abstract decoration.

In 1917, with more insights on Mondrian's works, Doesburg started to consciously add "abstraction" elements to his works. He drew representational sketches and slowly evolved the use of geometries in his works until the image in his paintings was beyond all recognition. His representative works in this period, *Rhythm of a Russian Dance* and *The Cow*, featured high degree of abstraction with evident characteristics of geometric elements. The composition was mainly the color blocks in forms of geometry, such as the rectangular, to simplify real objects until they were completely replaced by the abstract geometric shapes.

In 1918, Doesburg made a breakthrough in his abstract art by using grids with vertical and horizontal lines as the basis for composition, which brought new ideas to solve the problem between shapes and the background, and further integrated abstraction and geometry. *Composition in Gray* and *Composition in Dissonances* were among his representative works during this period.

From 1920 to 1924, Doesburg gave up painting and turned to architectural design and applied art. In late 1924, he began to paint again, and then created the series *Counter Composition* featuring square orthogonal format containing diagonal elements. The series appeared clear divergence between Doesburg and Mondrian in terms of how to use diagonal elements, which directly lead to the fact that the two masters went their separate ways as a direct consequence of the divergence.

forward

1917-1928
De Stijl

Piet Mondrian, the Source of Inspiration for De Stijl

The idea and expressive form of De Stijl originated from Mondrian's exploration of painting. Mondrian tried hard to express the power of nature and the mental state in painting under the influence of Van Gogh early in his career but later turned to Cubism after seeing the masterpieces of Picasso and Braque in 1911. After moving to Paris in 1912, he continued to explore the expression of Cubism, focusing on the structure and organization of paintings, to seek harmony and perfection through the balance of lines, colors, and segments. It occurred to him that Cubism failed to achieve "pure" expression, so he made years of exploration and gradually formed his own artistic ideas and ways, gradually shifting from the Cubist style to the pure and simple composition of abstract geometry.

Mondrian was forced to return to the Netherlands in 1914 due to the outbreak of the World War I, where he got into the theosophy under the influence of M. H. J. Schoenmaekers. With a great interest in the theosophy, Mondrian showed the inclination to geometric composition in the painting, and his paintings created in Paris and later in the Netherlands boasted increasing use of geometric elements. Afterward, he explored the abstract painting with only horizontal and vertical lines as the basic structure, and gradually reduced the colors to black and white and three primary colors, which made his paintings begin to show a high degree of rationality.

In 1916, Mondrian began to "process" visual materials including sea, beach, skyline, shoreline, and shoreside wharf, and abstracted them into geometric elements in his paintings. The abstract geometric composition was formed with crisscrossed horizontal and vertical lines. *Composition with Lines* and *Pier and Ocean* were vintage works by Mondrian in this period. Doesburg was, as it were, the driving force for Mondrian to develop his abstract style in a new direction, with his stained-glass windows design between 1916 and 1917 providing a framework for Mondrian.

Mondrian returned to Paris as the war ended in 1918. The free artistic atmosphere there enabled him to shape his geometric thinking. Trying to divide the picture into proportions according to a simple mathematical system, he created paintings composed on a grid to present the profound objective laws

of the universe with clear and regular artistic expression.

He believed it was excellent to use lines and colors to create the most essential beauty of rhythm and rhyme, and followed his intuition to construct his works. In his famous work *Lozenge with Grey Lines*, he applied a cubist layout with lines in it for the first time, which helped to constitute a stable square network. The rather concise geometric composition was in line with his pursuit of abstraction, while some other works used a diagonal grid as the layout. Between 1920 and 1921, he produced a series of paintings with asymmetrical composition.

The series of paintings he created later included the composition with red, yellow, blue, black, white and gray, which became representative works of De Stijl. Most people, when they thought of De Stijl, would have images of Mondrian's works in the 1920s in their minds: abstract geometric forms, asymmetrical compositions, pure primary-color squares on a white background with well-designed vertical and horizontal lines.

Mondrian proposed that artists be impersonal to depict natural objects with mathematical logic and then further abstract them into pure geometric forms, replace curves with vertical and horizontal lines to split images, and use geometric color blocks of red, yellow, and blue for asymmetric composition. His paintings have brought De Stijl new inspirations, with rigorous geometric composition influencing not only modern paintings but also modern graphic, architectural and industrial design.

1919 The Bauhaus

THE BAUHAUS

Many of the most avant-garde European artists came to Germany after the World War I, with the latest artistic concepts. The various ideological, artistic, and cultural exchanges enabled modernism to develop and gradually mature in Germany. In 1919, "Das Staatliches Bauhaus" (the Bauhaus) was established in Weimar with the active organization and planning of the famous architect Walter Gropius, by merging the Grand-Ducal Saxon Art School and the Grand Ducal Saxon School of Arts and Crafts, and Gropius was appointed as the dean. In the early 20th century, the Bauhaus ushered in a new era of modern design, forging ahead with bold innovation and exerting key influence on the design and style of modern art.

As the first school specializing in design education in the world, the Bauhaus attracted many art elites worldwide, including Wassily Kandinsky, Johannes Itten, Paul Klee, László Moholy-Nagy and Herbert Bayer. These artists made daring explorations and brand-new reforms in arts during their stay in the Bauhaus, allowing various artistic ideas to crash and generate new vitality.

Bauhaus in Weimar innovated the education of modern design by integrating teaching, research, and practice into an organic whole. As the Bauhaus entered its early glory days in Dessau with an increasing number of students, Gropius continued the well-developed teaching system built in Weimar, cultivating numerous talents who served as the pioneering designers of modernism later. After it moved to Berlin, it began to decline, and eventually ended up with closure. Although the Bauhaus lasted only 14 years with just over a thousand students, it had a profound impact on modernist art. It created the educational concept of modern design and made remarkable achievements in the theory and practice of art education.

The novel, objective, free, and perceptible geometric elements have always been the favorite of Bauhaus artists. Although the curriculum in the Bauhaus varied with different philosophies and expertise of the faculty, we can quickly see that the use of geometric elements, a concise and rational visual language, was brought to the attention of the artists throughout the development of the Bauhaus, and the works of its faculty or students show obvious geometrical characteristics.

The basic courses of the Bauhaus were lectured by artists such as Itten, Klee, Kandinsky, and Moholy-Nagy, who were quite enthusiastic about using geometric elements in artistic creation. It was assumed that children must be using the inborn vocabulary of visual communication. Children's drawings translate what they see into simple, generalized forms. They use lines, circles, squares and triangles. It certainly didn't seem like a coincidence that Euclid ordered and quantified physical

Johannes·Itten

space using lines and regular geometric forms — square, triangle, circle. Bauhaus designers came to assume that Euclidean shapes and pure, strong colors are the vocabulary of visual language.

Regardless of teachers' preference for geometric elements in theoretical guidance, or students' use of geometric shapes in course practice, geometric elements, as a rational and variable expression, had been running through the development of Bauhaus.

Bauhaus Weimar

Walter Gropius, the founder of the Bauhaus, proposed the slogan "Art and Technology — A New Unity" in view of the separation of art and technology under the condition of modern industrial production since the Industrial Revolution. For this purpose, he engaged three artists with different backgrounds: Lyonel Feininger, Gerhard Marcks, and Johannes Itten, among whom Itten made a great contribution to the development of the Bauhaus. From 1920 to 1922, Bauhaus employed a number of new masters, including Paul Klee, the German painter, and Wassily Kandinsky, the most important abstract art master at that time.

Bauhaus Weimar witnessed the establishment of new teaching systems, where the Bauhaus made bold reform of the classical teaching tradition, creating the dual-track education system and the apprenticeship system. In this period, the teaching curriculum was set and lectured in both artistic theory and technical practice. Each course was jointly undertaken by two masters: master of form was served by artists who mainly taught the knowledge of painting and inspired the creative thinking of students; master of craft mainly taught technology, handicraft art, and material science. This teaching system had nurtured a new generation of designers capable of modern artistic modeling, as well as mastering mechanical production and process technology.

The basic education curriculum in Weimar was of particular importance in the education reform of the Bauhaus, laying a solid foundation for the school. Itten, Klee, and Kandinsky analyzed visual art from a rational and scientific point of view and summarized some basic rules to be served as the basis for their teaching and guidance, making a great contribution to the building of education curriculum. In the teaching of basic courses, they had a great zest for using geometric shapes. They studied form, color, and composition from the basic key elements of dot, line, and plane, with the focus on the geometric elements, which directly made the graphic design break free from traditional painting and embrace scientific rationality. As the most direct expression of science and rationality, geometric elements, thus, got more widely used in graphic design.

Itten, Klee, and Kandinsky also did research on the relationship among color, form, and structure, including the abstract visual language and the geometry. They focused on the exploration of graphic design, thus developing a unique style in this genre. The Bauhaus developed visual vocabulary and color teaching system, contributing to the great improvement of the overall design and the public aesthetic in Germany, and enabling art to be more widely spread among the public.

Walter Gropius, the Father of the Bauhaus

At the very beginning, Walter Gropius, the founder of the Bauhaus, was dedicated to establishing a school of art and design. For him, the Bauhaus was a miniature Utopia where team spirit, social equality, and socialist ideals could be put into practice and the handicraft traditions would be given full play, with the purpose of benefiting the society through design and promoting intellectual exchange.

Gropius held that a new school of design must be formed to influence the national industrial circles. Therefore, he invited some radical artists to lecture in the Bauhaus to enrich and broaden the ideas and techniques of design. A new style of industrial arts and architecture came into being in the Bauhaus, emphasizing the practicability and giving full play to the technical and aesthetic properties of new materials and new structures. The new style featured flexible and diverse modeling with obvious geometric compositions and an orderly and concise layout.

Gropius believed that arts and handicrafts were not on the opposite sides but were two different aspects of the same activity. One of his core ideas of founding Bauhaus was to harmonize arts and crafts by education reforms. In accordance with his long-term ideal of achieving the coherence and unity of craft, technology, and art, the education of design should attach importance to the technical basis, while equal emphasis should be placed on the artistic creation, which together was also the center of the initial education reform. It was for this reason that he engaged both masters of form responsible for lecturing painting and masters of craft who taught craftsmanship, manufacturing techniques and material characteristics in workshops.

As a modern architect and architectural educator in Germany, Gropius created more works of architectural design than graphic design. However, his contribution to graphic design shall never be underestimated. In the Bauhaus, he taught students how to perceive things around them including color, form, size, texture, and mass, how to express the ideas as a designer uniquely while answering for practical standards, and how to maximize the function of a house or an appliance when it was put in certain forms and contours. His works showed quite distinct geometrical features.

Gropius introduced a new design style to the Bauhaus based on geometric lines. The factory he designed was no longer with any decoration. Instead, it was square with a flat roof, built with metal plates except for the pillars and inlaid with large glasses. Such a simple, light, and spacious factory met production demands perfectly. Moreover, the chair designed by Bauhaus was free of any decoration as well. The seatback was supported only by some wooden strips or steel bars in curve shapes. From teapot to buildings, Gropius taught his students to use the simplest geometry to create design patterns and styles with modern sense.

The most iconic work of Gropius in the 1920s was the Bauhaus schoolhouse that was designed according to his long-held principles of highlighting function, technology and economic benefits, as well as integrating art and technology. The concise and neat geometric design, the techniques of composition and the skills in dealing with architectural projects had been widely adopted in the later modernist architecture.

When designing the schoolhouse of the Bauhaus, Gropius highlighted such philosophies as asymmetry and contrasting. The cubes without any adornment appeared unusually vivid and lively thanks to the properly-calculated volumes, the well-arranged sizes, lengths, heights and locations, the contrast of the solid wall and the transparent glass, the clear distinction between the white wall and dark window frame, and the well-proportioned window, balcony, and awning. Asymmetrical shapes were used for the schoolhouse to set the overall flexibility off to the advantage, while geometric elements were incorporated in every design, in which the geometric shapes such as square glass windows and doors, spherical electric lights and round door handles can be seen everywhere. The geometry had made the schoolhouse filled with a simple and fresh air, as well as the rational and modern design.

Johannes Itten and His Courses

Johannes Itten was acclaimed as the greatest master of form in Bauhaus Weimar, whose main contribution was the designing of the Preparatory Course in the Bauhaus that was taught by himself. As he considered that the basic courses of design education should differ from the general painting courses, he designed a series of new courses centered on training the graphic visual sensitivity, i.e., the "Preparatory Course". As early as 1916, Itten consciously used geometric forms in his works and taught his students how to use such technique of expression in his Preparatory Course. His basic courses allowed the use of geometry to take root in the Bauhaus, supporting the school to develop with pure energy and vitality.

Walter Gropius
1883–1969

The themes of Itten's courses were divided into three categories: the study of natural objects and materials, the analysis of the works of masters in the early years, the research and sketching. In his Preparatory Course, he asked students to experience textures, shapes, colors, and hues, employ the elements in graphic and three-dimensional exercises, and analyze artistic works to grasp their inner spirit of the works and the content of expression. His students made a lot of practices on topics such as color, line, and diorama, exploring the fundamentals of visual experience and transforming the landscapes and human figures into such geometric elements as cylinders, spheres, and cubes. Or rather, they created new human figures and landscapes with geometric forms.

Other than the above studies, he taught theories on contrasting, forms, and colors. His teaching of formalism emphasized the perception and application of geometric elements, so he started by expounding on the features of geometric elements, and explained that there was a necessary inner relationship between shapes like square, circle and triangle, and colors since the circle was circular featuring "fluidity" and "centrality", the square was horizontal and vertical featuring "stability", and the triangle boasting "obliquity". Therefore, he emphasized the combination of color training and geometry training as soon as he served as master of form.

In addition, his students were instructed to make spheres, cubes, pyramids, cones, and cylinders with clay, and create works conforming to the features of some specific geometric form so as to perceive the three-dimensional space and basic geometric forms. Itten believed that only through these connections can the geometric expression of three-dimensional space look vivid and real in the light and shade contrast, and can the students grasp and skillfully use geometry to achieve the illusion of spatial depth on planes.

The teaching programs of the Bauhaus in the following years proved that the forming concepts on color basis and form basis were particularly important in design. Paul Klee took Itten's courses and later incorporated these concepts into his teaching.

Paul Klee's Courses

Paul Klee joined the Bauhaus without much teaching experience, and most of his knowledge and skills in teaching were acquired through self-study. As one of the few artists who enjoyed extensive reading, Klee was quite interested in theoretical issues and devoted himself to simplifying and clarifying art theories. He believed that all complex organic forms evolved from simple basic forms, and learning about how the natural forms took shape was an essential precondition for the mastery of the complex natural forms.

Klee was widely recognized as one of the most important expressionist artists, whose art reflected the spirit of the age. He proposed that circle, triangle and square were the three basic geometric forms, and the artistic works were created based on the variable relations of these basic geometric elements.

Klee's preference for mathematics and physics can be seen in his teaching ideas and works. He favored rational expression and held that mathematics and physics pushed the artists to focus on the functions rather than the final form of expression. The algebra, geometry, physics, and such prompted Bauhaus education to develop towards nature and functionality instead of impressiveness. Therefore, Klee proposed to see through the appearance to perceive the essence, and to learn to dig into the root of the problem and make it clear with analysis.

Even though Klee set his basic courses based on scientific theories, he gave lectures with more emphasis on the relationship between feeling and creativity. He believed that there was an intrinsic link between lines and colors. He gave symbolic meaning to points, lines, and forms, and laid stress on the interdependence and integration of all forms.

About 30 students were taking his class during the early days, some of whom recalled that in class Klee would require them to focus on practicing the techniques of using simple shapes such as squares, circles, and triangles, and relating them to each other. Klee's courses were designed based on the study of basic forms and later enriched by introducing basic colors piece by piece, to inspire a sense of graphic composition and explore the infinite potential of design. Art could be made boundless with the use of such techniques as proportion, rotation, and reflection, in combination with color theory.

Klee had a rather better command of geometry in his *Red Balloon*, *The Messenger of Autumn*, *Growth of The Night Plants*, and such, in which the influence of Cubist painting on him was blindingly obvious. *Red Balloon* featured quite distinct geometrical elements. The tree, balloon and the building were depicted in geometric forms. As an abstract expression, pure geometry was endowed with symbolic meaning here. It was the visual tension that created a unique artistic charm in these works as well as his *Rope Dancer* created later in 1923, in which the performance equipment that was composed of geometric elements stole all the spotlights from the facial feature of the dancer. The use of geometric elements was quite entertaining and unique, revealing Klee's belief in artistic creation that artists were required to systematically learn about graphic elements so as to intuitively use them to achieve the desired effect.

Klee once said, "Art does not reproduce what we see; rather, it makes us see." The nature of graphic art drew artists close to abstraction, then to represent what we saw in an abstract way, and further to reveal something different. For him, abstraction was to create with simple geometric shapes such as squares, triangles, and circles as graphic elements. Although he incorporated the graphic elements of graphic art in his works, he realized that they shall not be the only elements involved.

Wassily Kandinsky, the Master of Abstract Art

Wassily Kandinsky joined the Bauhaus in 1922 at the climax of his artistic creation as a master of form in the Mural Painting Workshop and also taught formalism theory in the basic theoretical course as well. Like Klee, he adopted the systematic teaching method and, with synthesis and analysis as the starting point, set up the basic courses of design strictly on a scientific and rational basis. As the first true abstract painter, Kandinsky played a rather positive role in promoting the development of Bauhaus.

As far as Walter Gropius was concerned, artists should broaden horizons that are essential for creating a brand-new kind of design capable of serving the modern society. He also believed that it was of necessity to offer theoretical courses for students to better learn about form, and insisted that "free art" should be the basis of practical art.

Moreover, Kandinsky taught a specialized course, Analytical Painting, in Bauhaus. In this course, his students were required to make still life of ordinary household utensils or objects of the studio, analyze the shapes and relationships of those objects from the perspective of geometry,

and keep copying some combined elements and basic lines until they finished an abstract yet harmonious painting. Through such assignments Kandinsky showed his analysis of still life to his students. Later in Dessau, Kandinsky performed a more systematic study of Analytical Painting. The clear straight lines and shapes in his works may give credit for the structural geometry of analytic painting.

Considering that Kandinsky shared the same philosophy with Itten in terms of color and form, his courses, as it were, followed Itten's teaching philosophy but failed to make a breakthrough. Color theory was not Itten's focus, while Kandinsky paid more attention to the details between form and color in his color course, which just filled the gap.

By emphasizing the specific use of form and color in design, Kandinsky guided students to design a "single part" of form and color in the first place, and then made various combinations to study the visual effects arising from matching the parts. Kandinsky started with the three primary colors (red, yellow, and blue) and the basic shapes (circle, triangle, and square), and then endowed each shape and color with a specific role, allowing such common elements as color and graphic composition to bring about expressive effects in the combination. He believed that there were intrinsic links between forms and colors, which would emerge with appropriate matching, such as "yellow triangle, blue circle, and red square".

All these showed Kandinsky's scientific criteria for art throughout his career, and life-long exploration of art as a science. Such philosophy had been running through his teaching in the Bauhaus and artistic creation as well, producing a positive effect of expression he valued so much. He insisted that students should learn how to systematically use these elements before creative design.

The Bauhaus aimed to establish its theoretical system of visual elements that would serve as a basis for both art and design in practice, to promote cooperation and create an inclusive environment for design. The faculty all contributed to this goal with their teaching program and artistic creation. Kandinsky was one of them, developing his theory and constantly progressing in his artistic creation. In 1923, Kandinsky created a series of works signifying his geometric expression that had taken shape since 1919, including the *Composition* series, *On White (II)*, and *Orange*. These works featured a rather coherent style of geometric abstraction, displaying the elements he drew from the Russian avant-garde while retaining his consistent composition with richness and complexity, i.e., the combination of big colored blocks and thick black lines, the composition segmented by thick lines, the irregular forms overlapping with colors, the curving lines in concert with colors, the use of such pure geometric elements as circle, square, and triangle, etc.

The Bauhaus shared many features with De Stijl as for the design philosophy. The purpose of establishing the Bauhaus was to break the boundary between artists and craftsmen, form a brand-new organization of designers, and change the society by reforming art education. On the other hand, the artists of De Stijl shouldered the responsibilities of social reform and the anti-war movement, intending to reform the art by winning over the social forces beyond the art circle, and then promoted the reform in art fields including architecture and design. Therefore, the ideals of De Stijl were echoed by the Bauhaus, speeding up the education reform of the latter.

The Bauhaus had drawn upon the achievements of the then modernist design in Europe, especially of the Russian Constructivism. Meanwhile, De Stijl exerted great influence on the development of the Bauhaus, with the founder Doesburg contributing the most. He, together with other artists of De Stijl, made close contact and exchanges with the colleagues in the Bauhaus, which promoted the development of modernist design in Europe.

In November 1920 when Doesburg visited the Bauhaus, he was impressed by its teaching activities, and soon decided to get the magazine *De Stijl* published in Bauhaus Weimar. The vast experiment in modern design education was quite appealing to him. Doesburg, as one of the pioneers who ushered in early modernism, emphasized the use of basic geometry, especially the square structure formed by perpendicular lines and square colored facets, which was a guiding principle for modernist art and design. The influence of De Stijl on the Bauhaus in early phases was reflected in the armchair designed by Marcel Breuer in 1922 which incorporated its cantilever design into the vertical structure and showcased the aesthetics of the Bauhaus.

In addition to the product design, the layout design of the Bauhaus was also deeply influenced by De Stijl. For example, the cover of the Bauhaus admission brochure in 1923 shared a similar style with that of the magazine *De Stijl* in 1921. In addition, most of the well-known Bauhaus publications were designed by Moholy-Nagy under the influence of De Stijl.

The Workshops of the Bauhaus Weimar

The Bauhaus Weimar encouraged the designers to return to the world of technology for the revival of the craft tradition. After finishing the basic courses, students had access to one of Bauhaus workshops to learn craftsmanship, including The Pottery

Workshop, The Weaving Workshop, The Metal Workshop, The Furniture Workshop, The Stained Glass and Mural Painting Workshop, The Stone-sculpting and Wood-carving Workshop, The Bookbinding Workshop, The Graphic Printing Workshop, and The Theatre Workshop. With the instruction from both artists and craftsmen, students would acquire comprehensive knowledge, which was conducive to their creation of works that blend craftsmanship and aesthetics.

For the Bauhaus, geometry was always superior to any mass production. The use of geometric elements was valued by the Bauhaus faculty and students not only in the artist-led basic courses but also in the process of learning and practice in the workshops.

The Pottery Workshop encouraged students to shape the pottery themselves. The geometric shapes such as cone, cylinder, sphere and circle were the most common elements present in most of their works.

In the Weaving Workshop, students creatively experimented with new methods to create new patterns and forms in riotous profusion, which could not be done without the guidance of artists. They tended to incorporate basic geometry and various combinations of primitive colors into their works and drew inspiration from the basic shapes and such "formalism languages" they learned in the classes of Itten.

The Metal Workshop focused on creating vessels for daily use including jar, urn, candlestick, pot, and box, with basic geometry such as circle and sphere, for the most part, some of which followed the golden ratio as well. The lamps and lanterns were mostly characterized by a circular base, cylindrical shaft, and spherical shade. The metal products designed in Bauhaus were made up of regular geometric solids, featuring some tranquility and uniformity borrowed from the articles of manufacture.

The geometric elements were more widely used in the Furniture Workshop where almost every piece of design was marked by geometric shapes — the square chair back, the square dresser with circular mirror, the spherical handle of table drawer, and the triangular holders steadily placed. In 1922, Peter Keler, a student of Bauhaus, showed a new approach in his designing of cradle, with innovation not only in the new interpretation of the design but also in the form of expression. The cradle blended the basic geometric shape and the three primary colors. Its hollow triangular prism, upended for baby to sleep in, had red sides and two yellow triangle bottoms with a blue circumcircle each used for rocking the cradle. The combination of the basic geometric shape and the three primary colors was quite influenced by the design concept of Kandinsky.

It was the Graphic Printing Workshop that was most closely related to the development of graphic design among all workshops in the Bauhaus Weimar. With the support of Gropius, Lyonel Feininger, a master of form of the Graphic Printing Workshop, took on the printing of all graphic works by the faculty and students. The graphic masters of the Bauhaus devoted themselves to exploring the design style characterized by geometric elements and kept creating graphic artworks, some of which were printed by the Graphic Printing Workshop, including Feininger's *Twelve Woodcuts* series and Kandinsky's *Small Worlds* series. The workshop also printed the *Bauhaus Masters' Portfolio*, a collection of the works of all the artists who taught at the Bauhaus at the time. In addition, Joost Schmidt designed the poster for the Bauhaus Exhibition. The poster was structured with obliquely crossed vertical and horizontal lines, and the squares and circles were decomposed and recombined to form a large geometric composition in the simple and multilayered style with special visual effects, embodying its achievements in the abstract geometry.

BAUHAUS
1919-1933

Bauhaus Dessau

As the right-wing forces gained more momentum, Gropius announced the closure of the Bauhaus Weimar in March 1925. His real purpose was staying aloof from the political vortex in Weimar and looking for somewhere else more suitable for the development of the Bauhaus.

Gropius chose Dessau in the end to relocate the Bauhaus, where he served as director for another three years, and Bauhaus ushered in a formative period for its teaching system and reached another pinnacle. In 1926, the Bauhaus added the "Academy of Design" to its name, building the distinct link between design and the Bauhaus for the first time. However, the great change was that it had its new department — department of architecture — in the period.

Gropius announced his resignation in 1928 without any signs, leaving the faculty and students unprepared. He explained that considering the smooth operation of the Bauhaus he decided to put more of his time and energy into the architecture. Hannes Meyer took the position in the same year and initiated the internal restructuring. However, due to his political standpoints, there were rather few words about his teaching in the Bauhaus in history, and he was often called the unknown Bauhaus director. In August 1930, Meyer was discharged from his post by the Dessau authorities for fear of losing precious votes occupied by communist students.

Ludwig Mies van der Rohe became his successor when the Bauhaus was undergoing the most difficult period. In 1931, the extreme right wings were growing rapidly in Germany and the Nazi Party was seizing power. The political situation made the development of Bauhaus more and more difficult, and its political support gained from the local government came to an end as soon as the Nazis took control of the Dessau City Council.

The Bauhaus Dessau witnessed its maturity in art and the formation of its style in graphic design under the influence of both De Stijl and Russian Constructivism. Therefore, the graphic design featured high rationalization, functionalization, simplification, minimalism, and geometry. Herbert Bayer and László Moholy-Nagy had made the greatest impact.

In this period, Bauhaus published its journal, *Bauhaus*, as the main ground for its experiments on graphic design. Moholy-Nagy was responsible for this publication's graphic design and layout design for all the covers and most of the pages except for two issues. Herbert Bayer was also deeply involved in the design of *Bauhaus*. They widely adopted simple geometric shapes and structures, sans serifs, and concise layouts. Moreover, Moholy-Nagy was in charge of the layout design for other publications in the period.

László Moholy-Nagy, the Master of Constructivism in Bauhaus

Moholy-Nagy, who introduced Constructivism to Bauhaus, was skilled in incorporating his ideas of modern art in designs. He had a key influence on the academy and ranked first in Bauhaus in terms of graphic design. After joining the Bauhaus, he took over the duties of Itten, working as a master in the Metal Workshop while teaching basic courses. He removed all the religious content emphasized by Itten, as well as those highlighting personal emotions and self-improvement.

His courses were designed to let students master the form and content of the expression techniques, the materials, the graphic design, and the cubism, as well as the basic scientific principles related to color, trying to shift the focus from personal artistic expression to the understanding and mastery of new technologies and media. His students have followed his instructions to do their metalworks and created works with both abstract yet simple geometric shapes, as well as definite and appropriate functions and characteristics. Moholy-Nagy was adept at the abstract processing of specific images by magnifying details or exploring unusual angles, which was later used in graphic design works, enabling the graphic design to boast a sense of modern.

Influenced by the constructivist artists Vladimir Tatlin and Lissitzky, Moholy-Nagy's ideological concepts and working methods were closely related to Constructivism, which he applied in graphic design, painting, experimental film, product design, and furniture design. The design and creation were all done by himself, which played a key role in adjusting the development of the Bauhaus.

Moholy-Nagy made a great contribution to graphic design. Most of his works were abstract, made up of simple geometric shapes, in which the sense of form was fully expressed in the variety of geometric shapes and abstract lines. He was also keen to use contrasting colors to enhance the impact of the image. Significantly, he was quite skilled at expressing the sense of space, and widely used the technique in various graphic designs.

Moholy-Nagy had delivered many graphic works, especially the book designs, for the Academy and other units when working in Bauhaus. With the emphasis on the asymmetrical balance and the rigorous style of the geometric structure free of decoration, his designs featured briefness, a distinct theme, and a strong sense of contemporaneity. He believed in the strength of simple structures, and expressed it in graphic designs. The Bauhaus series and posters he designed, as well as the photographs he took, made full use of simple geometric elements including the basic geometric shapes and structures. Thanks to the abstract geometry, his designs had a strong sense of rationality which exerted a positive influence on the field. Such design philosophy and approaches provided new insights for his students.

His works enriched the sense of space by distorting the perspective of geometric forms to express three-dimensionality in sharp contrast with the background. In terms of his *Construction* series, the geometric figures such as quadrilaterals, circles, and triangles overlapped one another in these abstract paintings had created a sense of space, allowing the viewer to sense the three-dimensional and variable structure and enhancing perspective. He once said, "I wanted to eliminate all factors which might disturb their clarity — in contrast, for example, with Kandinsky's paintings, which reminded me sometimes of an undersea world. My desire was to work with the peculiar characteristics of colors, with their pure relationships. I chose simple geometrical forms as a step towards such objectivity."

In the Bauhaus Dessau, Moholy-Nagy shouldered the responsibility of the cover designs and layout designs for almost all publications, including his *Von Material zu Architektur* and Gropius' *Bauhausbauten Dessau* in 1930. The quarterly *Bauhaus*, the first official journal, was designed under his charge by and large. Characterized by basic geometric shapes and structures as concise as possible, together with the abstract composition of graphic elements and the simple color matching, these works showed a free and abstract visual effect.

Herbert Bayer, the Master of Graphic Design

As one of the most important figures in the modern design of the 20th century, Herbert Bayer had special talents in graphic design, exhibition design, architectural design, painting, and photography. In 1921, he went to Weimar for study in the Bauhaus, learning from Kandinsky and Moholy-Nagy. He later took charge of the Graphic Printing Workshop from 1925 to 1928, a period in which he had a great interest in advertising technology and designed a number of works, and meanwhile, he dedicated himself to the study of typographic design and layout design.

In 1926, he designed a series of sans serif named Universal Typeface, in which he removed the extra decorative lines and introduced such simple geometric shapes as circles and lines to express the form of the alphabet, which had a more concise structure suitable for message delivery and exchange and got widely used in Bauhaus publications.

Meanwhile, Bayer advocated Structural Design Language for the layout design, in which simple lines or geometric shapes were used to divide a layout and convey information through the hierarchical visual structure. For example, the poster Bayer designed for Kandinsky's 60th birthday in 1926 was composed of rotated and divided pictures with various sizes of fonts and lines to realize a dynamically-balanced visual information hierarchy while emphasizing the layout order.

Bayer pursued functional design and a high degree of simplicity without ornamentation and learned from Constructivism to achieve structural integrity with the geometric models, making his works marked with scientificity and rationality. As for the layout design, Bayer preferred the concise and generalized graphic features, the space divided by points, lines, planes, and volumes, the dynamic composition composed of horizontal lines, vertical lines, and oblique lines, as well as the asymmetric forms, all of which constituted his style of poster design for the Bauhaus. He attempted to go after the style of his teacher, Doesburg, to make the geometric division of the picture in the proportion of space. The De Stijl, keen on the composition of geometry, space, and color, was skilled in using vertical and horizontal geometry, primary color, and neutral color time and again, which impressed Bayer a lot.

Beyer was inclined to express the images with alternative visual effects and symbolic techniques. He would use squares, circles, triangles, and other geometric shapes in his creation. In 1926, he designed the poster for Professor Hans' photography lecture with a simple and readable style by matching the rational geometric elements with the sans serif.

As for the cover of the first issue of *Bauhaus* in 1928, Bayer used projections of cones, spheres, triangles, and cubes as design elements, and expressed a strong sense of rationalist design by enlarging the details and presenting them from special angles. Bayer designed the cover of its fourth issue later this year, with a large circle placed in the most prominent position and a picture in the center depicting young male and female students lying together with their heads towards the circle center. It created a sense of unity and positivity, showing the charm of the Bauhaus where young artists from all over the world gathered to learn design together.

On the recommendation of Gropius, Ludwig Mies van der Rohe, one of the most important masters in modernist architectural design, took over as Bauhaus director in August 1930. Based on his life-long artistic practice, he established the style of modernist architecture and proposed the guiding principle — "less is more". He influenced generations of modern designers and thus revolutionized architectures of the world, which were such marvelous achievements that very few could make.

At the very beginning of being the director, however, he was confronted with opposition from many Bauhaus students who accused him of being a "formalist", that is, people who only designed the luxury mansion for the privileged few and had no regard for the dwellings for the poor. Some even doubted his design capability and required him to display his designs in the academy to qualify himself for leadership. Some opposition was from the faculty, such as Kandinsky and Josef Albers, who complained about the theoretical courses and demanded more teachers in sociology, economics, and psychology.

It was under such difficult circumstances that Mies van der Rohe took charge of the Bauhaus. In response to the severe situation, he had no choice but to put the academy in good order over his autocratic leadership. He transformed the Bauhaus into an architectural academy where students had access to some workshops, and the compulsory basic courses were classified as electives. Compared to Meyer, he laid far less emphasis on functionalism. As an architect, he was fastidious about the form of architecture and refused to sacrifice formal beauty for function.

Although Mies van der Rohe preferred to design in the geometric style with linear features, it was structure and technique that mattered for the most part. As for the public buildings and museums, he was proficient at designing in symmetry, frontality, and side depiction; while for the residential buildings, such methods as asymmetry, fluidity, and interlocking were mainly used. Whatever the design style was, his works were characterized by rational minimalism and the use of geometric shapes or lines to divide the space.

Apart from purging the left-wing of the academy, he focused on reforming the teaching system to consolidate the foundation of architectural design for the development of the Bauhaus. Under his leadership, architectural education had been the priority, and the Bauhaus had changed beyond recognition in its last few years, with its curricula, its pedagogical methods, and its ideological basis contrary to the initial purpose put forward by Gropius. Therefore, most of the masters involved in the initial educational experiments resigned from the academy one after another, leaving only a few old faculty members, such as Kandinsky and Klee. Soon after Mies van der Rohe took office, Klee resigned, and Kandinsky was left with little to do, for most of the art courses were called off.

Bauhaus Berlin

In September 1932, the Dessau authority announced the closure of the Bauhaus. On 30 September, the Nazis raided the academy, marking a hasty end of the Bauhaus Dessau, which was considered a key stage in Bauhaus history. Mies van der Rohe had decided a few months earlier to move the Bauhaus to Berlin as a private-run academy and renamed it the "Bauhaus Independent Teaching and Research Institute" with a new subtitle added. Finally, the new campus was relocated to an abandoned telephone company building in Steglitz, Berlin.

In January 1933, the Nazi government seized the power and Hitler became the Chancellor of Germany. The German Ministry of Culture issued the first order in April to close the Bauhaus. On 19 July, Mies van der Rohe called the masters together and gave an account of the financial and political situation and then proposed dissolving the Bauhaus. This was approved by all present. Although taken in a context of extreme political and financial tribulation, this decision nevertheless represented one final exercise in the intellectual freedom of choice.

The Bauhaus had been struggling for development in its short and tough history from 1919 to 1933, and still received long-standing attention after dissolution, which was a tribute to what it had achieved over the past 14 years. However, some people would misunderstand or tend to evaluate the development of Bauhaus in an oversimplified or prejudiced view. Given this, careful analysis and discernment were required as the influence of Bauhaus permeated every aspect of design.

Its most important and significant influence on graphic design was the establishment of the basic system of design education encompassing graphic composition, three-dimensional composition, and color composition. In the second place, the Bauhaus enriched the design theory by pointing out that design should be made on the geometric grid layout, which would make the graphic design simple, functional, accurate, geometric, and highly rational. Artists of the Bauhaus innovatively inherited and developed the application of geometric elements in graphic design, creating a classic trend. Until today, the basic geometric shapes are still the indispensable elements for the trendy classic works in graphic design.

1950 Beyond the Bauhaus

BEYOND THE BAUHAUS

As modern graphic design was heading to maturity with a series of artistic styles and Bauhaus design ideology, the use of geometric elements in graphic design had achieved great and continuous development in Bauhaus in spite of its closure in 1933. From Switzerland to the United States, and to Japan, the development of modern graphic design, with the interaction of various factors, enjoyed good momentum towards maturity. The rich diversity and differences kept emerging in the practice, and infinite possibilities and potential had been revealed during the process of applying geometric elements in graphic design.

International Typographic Style

The spirit of Swiss graphic design lies in its neatness, rigor, practicability, geometrization, and rationality. Although it was not until the 1950s that the International Typographic Style was established, the meticulous and accurate style was all the rage worldwide, exerting the greatest influence among the post-war graphic design styles. It was also the most popular style around the globe. Therefore, it was also referred to as the International Typographic Style.

Closely tied to the Bauhaus and the De Stijl, this style was characterized by the efforts to achieve design unity through a simple grid structure, almost standardized formula layout, and concise geometric expression. Such a geometric visual language was quite advantageous to internationalize communication. The International Typographic Style has exerted wide influence around the world, being the most important global graphic design style. Theo Ballmer and Max Bill, the two Swiss graphic designers graduating from the Bauhaus, were the key figures in the International Typographic Style.

Theo Ballmer learned design from Paul Klee, Walter Gropius, and Hannes Meyer in Bauhaus Dessau, where he attempted to integrate the De Stijl into graphic design and standardize the vertical and horizontal layout with the simple geometric mathematical formula. In 1928, the posters he designed made a hit, with the characteristics of the vertical and horizontal grid layout, distinct geometries, and strong sense of modern. Taking "büro", the poster he designed for an architectural exhibition in Basel, Switzerland as an example, its graphic design with the layout expressing direct and clear-cut messages stood out, since the vertical and horizontal layout put the words in the structured grid, and the four letters of "büro" were designed with obvious geometric features.

Max Bill, as a versatile designer occupied in various fields, had richer professional experience compared to Theo Ballmer. He studied in the Bauhaus from 1927 to 1929 under the tutelage of Gropius, Kandinsky, Moholy-Nagy, Meyer and so on. His layout was based on mathematical proportions, standard proportions of geometric shapes, and frequent use of sans serifs. For the first step, he divided the graphic space into several simple functional areas with vertical and horizontal lines as the center and then used simple geometric squares to form the grids, each of which was taken as the basic unit. Next, he made the layout according to mathematical proportion and geometric proportion and highlighted the geometric expression in design.

The Modern Graphic Design in America

A large number of artists immigrated to the United States after the World War II, contributing to the development of modern design in the US. The introduction of the International Typographic Style caused a sensation instantly. Large enterprises in the US, which became the economic superpower after the World War II, embarked on global economic expansion as early as the 1950s, so there was an urgent need for a graphic design style that could facilitate global communication. The arrival of the International Typographic Style was like a timely rain in the right place at the right time, and it was widely recognized and used in the United States by virtue of its rigorous, practical, geometric, rational characteristics.

The International Typographic Style had been popular in the United States for more than 20 years since the 1950s, with the Graphic Design Office at the MIT exerting the most profound influence. The Office insisted on using the geometric grid network as the basic structure of the design, standardizing all the complex graphics, words, and illustrations in the network to make the design achieve a high degree of geometrization and rigor. The Office designed a large number of education-related posters largely based on abstract graphic shapes and with the use of simple combinations of typefaces, geometric shapes, or geometric variations, for a strong graphic effect.

Saul Bass, as one of the most important masters of American graphic design in the 20th century, brought modern graphic design from New York to Los Angeles. Bass was skillful in extracting and creating graphics with symbolic and associative meanings from the concrete objects. After moving to Los Angeles, Bass took on the poster design for a large number of Hollywood movies. He abandoned the specific and straightforward images in the traditional movie posters and dedicated himself to extracting the storyline for the creation of abstract figures. In 1955, Bass designed the poster for the film *The Man with the Golden Arm*, with rough rectangles as a frame of the poster and an abstract arm composed of highly-distorted geometric shapes in the center.

As a versatile artist and designer of extraordinary ability, Bass designed visual images for many enterprises in the United States, and made films as director and producer. The variety of practice endowed his graphic works with an extraordinary style. He was capable of making graphic designs out of diversified media comprehensively.

Bradbury Thompson was also an influential graphic designer in the United States. His design was full of experimentation and exploration and defied all principles of simple rationalism. He preferred decorative typefaces of different styles, and incorporated them into geometric shapes by means of contrast. His designs made extensive use of geometric shapes and dynamic layout, and his use of colors features a high degree of freedom.

Despite the above distinctive characteristics, he still stressed the basic structure with the geometric vertical and horizontal layout and highlighted the clarity of visual communication, which was essentially an attempt to unify the basic principles of the Swiss style with the vivid American design. His experiment aroused widespread interest in the field of design of the United States.

After the World War II, large enterprises in the United States went into the international market for development and expansion, and thus started to create a corporate image of their own. Under such special conditions, the design of corporate visual identity had matured in the United States, laying the foundation for corporations in countries around the world to design their images in the future.

In the 1960s, Chermayeff & Geismar Associates took the lead in the corporate identity design in the United States, which created corporate images for many large US corporations that were internationally influential, such as those for Chase Manhattan Bank. Chermayeff & Geismar Associates made a thorough research on the operations and customers of the Bank in combination with the characteristics of New York City and then created a whole corporate identity system that included a corporate logo, desired typefaces, color pallets, and usage specification. As for the corporate logo, they used four trapezoids to make up the regular octagon, leaving a blank square space in the middle. The abstract technique of expression broke through the limitation of corporate image design at that time and got rid of the design method that highlighted only letters or figurative graphics.

The corporate identity design of Exxon Mobil was regarded as another world-famous masterpiece of the Chermayeff & Geismar Associates. With thoughtful research, it came up with a very simple design: a rectangular base with the name "Mobil" in the concise sans serif above it. The layout of the five letters made the longitudinal lines more prominent, so the emphasis was on the five vertical lines, highlighting capital letter "M". The letter "o" and the lower right part of the letter "b" were designed into a circle, whose geometric processing made the overall design full of visual tension as well as neatness. The color matching of the letters was also very characteristic. All the letters were blue except for the red "o", creating a good visual impact.

Saul Bass had also been actively involved in corporate identity design. He believed that such kind of design should have a distinct connotation for people to understand the enterprise via its image design, and should be easy to be remembered. Therefore, he tended to use geometric shapes with symbolic meanings to create both concise and vivid designs.

In 1984, Bass was commissioned to design the corporate identity image for AT&T, which was separated from its parent company, the Bell Telephone Company. Bass was required to replace its image of "national phone company" with "global telephone company", so he abandoned the original Bell-shaped logo, and used the circle as the basic form run through by the dotted horizontal lines to form a highlight, so that the circle looked like a sphere, creating the specific image of the concept of "global".

The Modern Graphic Design in Japan

Japan, an economic power emerging after the war, has a narrow territory and dense population, boosting a strong sense of graphic design since ancient times. Its illustrations, woodcut printed posters (Ukiyo-e), and various traditional packaging are quite influential in the world.

In the 1950s, the awareness of design in the Japanese government and the people was greatly enhanced, and famous designers from Europe and the United States were frequently invited to Japan to give lectures and guidance. With a comprehensive understanding of modernist design in Europe and the United States, as well as many aesthetic similarities between their own rational design and European constructivism, Japanese artists, especially graphic designers, had a special liking for constructivism. The rigorous analysis and use of geometric structures, especially vertical and horizontal structures in constructivist design and art, fascinated them, but Japanese designers tended to favor symmetrical layouts rather than asymmetric constructivist compositions.

Traditional Japanese culture had a strong preference for vertical and horizontal lines as well as simple geometric shapes, which explained why post-war Japanese graphic designers became interested in European constructivism.

In the 1960s, with the rapid and steady economic growth, Japanese design entered a development period. Products such as automobiles and home appliances had won wide recognition in the international market for the high quality and relatively low price. Industrial development and the increasing cultural exchanges had made the design more important. Moreover, various product exhibitions and design exchange activities had been organized in Japan. During this period, Japanese graphic designers, represented by Yusaku Kamekura and Kazumasa Nagai, began to form their unique design style, which attracted the attention of the global graphic designers. The development of Japanese graphic design showed an unstoppable tendency with overwhelming force. In the subsequent two decades, Japanese graphic design ushered in a booming period.

With his series of posters designed for the Tokyo Olympic Games in 1964, Yusaku Kamekura made Japanese poster design emerge on the world stage. His major works include the poster for the 18th Olympic Games, the poster for the Osaka Expo, and the logos and signs designed for the Nippon Telephone and Telegraph. He was quite rigorous in designs and in the control of printing technology, creating works with distinct personal characteristics. His works featured a strong sense of geometry and modern, as well as symbolism and simplicity embodied in the traditional Japanese family emblem.

It can be said that the Japanese poster design in the 1960s developed from a unified basic plan, which led directly to the emerging of new modeling in the form of concrete images rather than an ideological assumption. The repeated application showed that the concept and practice had been mature, on which the designers had built confidence. As a result, they started to go with their instinct, helping the Japanese design style to take shape. Yusaku Kamekura, through his exuberant creation which was full of enthusiasm, provided a way for post-war poster design in Japan.

Kazumasa Nagai, another representative figure of Japanese graphic design, witnessed the development and transition of Japanese graphic design from the establishment of the Japan Advertising Artists Club after the war to the gradual acceptance of Japanese graphic design by the public, as well as the important role the new designs played in the economic take-off of Japan. His designs are full of his own style. His pursuit of the abstract form of expression, which he said was influenced by Yusaku Kamekura, remains unchanged.

He tended to find the rational elements among the simple vertical and horizontal lines, to form a new graphic design with photography and illustration included. His use of vertical and horizontal lines, including the standard unit, namely the module unit, was similar to the systematic design of Ulm School of Design and Braun in Germany at that time, which was also a very typical internationalist design method. In fact, his internationalism originated from the traditional decoration and design of the Japanese folk. For example, his poster for *Tradition et Nouvelles Techniques*, an exhibition of works by Japanese graphic designers in 1984 in Paris, used simple geometric shapes to create a strong visual impact that was widely praised in Western design circles.

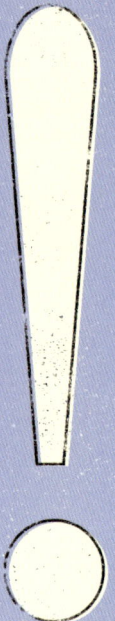

NOW! A–Z

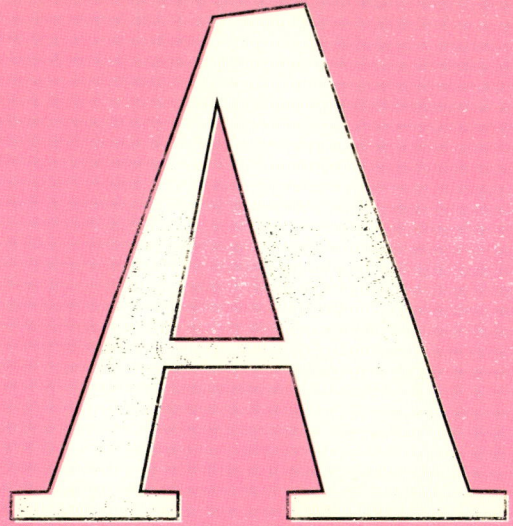

THE MORE ABSTRACT IS FORM, THE MORE CLEAR AND DIRECT IS ITS APPEAL. — WASSILY KANDINSKY

ABSTRACT

andSons

Base was tasked with creating a timeless and iconic brand identity, and a set of high-end collectible packaging that reflect the brand's inherent tensions: tradition and innovation; refinement and generosity; luxury and surprise. The playful yet elegant identity system embodies the vision of the brand — a new perspective on fine chocolate. Each box features a different custom-drawn shape. The color palette is bright but also delicate, evoking the sunshine of L.A. while conveying an elevated and luxurious feeling.

Designer Arno Baudin, Gabriela Carnabuci, Gina Shin | Studio Base Design | Client andSons Chocolatiers

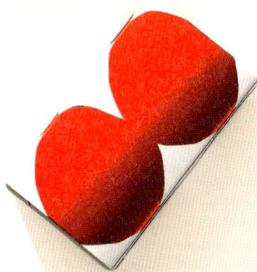

Still Life Exhibit

Based on such elements as fruits, flowers and water vessels, the designer hoped to interpret the beauty of inanimate objects. So she presented the items in various arrangements — fruits and flowers are in geometric shapes, and water vessels are presented in a figurative way.

Designer Zhu Peihua

Geometry Now !

靜 STILL
爭 LIFE
物 展

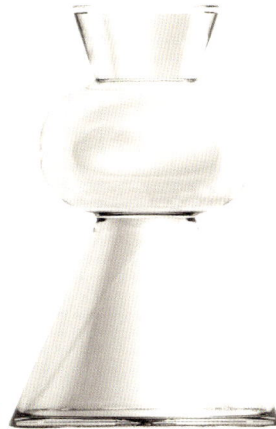

許多事物都有其象徵意義，主要是取決於是否感受到這些事物的美。

Still Life exhibit
KAOHSIUNG
2018.06.07-14
三餘書店 TaKaoBooks

TOUMEI ✕ Carolina Spencer ✕ 田井將博

時間：每日10:00-17:00 (16:30後停止售票)
詳細活動資訊：https://en.cksmh.gov/

886-2-2343-1100

静 物 展

STILL LIFE

許多事物都有其象徵意義，主要是取決於感受到這些事物的美。

Still Life exhibit
TAIPEI
2018.04.19-26
朋丁 PON DING 2F

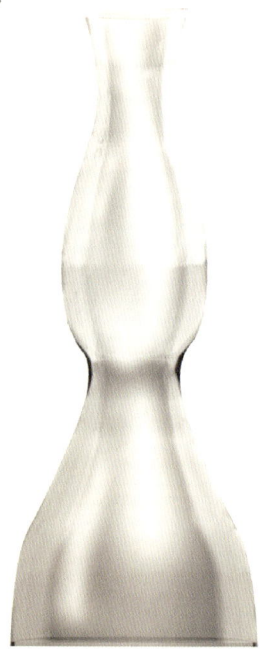

TOUMEI ✕ Carolina Spencer ✕ 田井將博

時間：每日10:00-17:00 (16:30後停止售票)
詳細活動資訊：https://en.cksmh.gov/

886-2-2343-1100

Still Life exhibit
TAICHUNG
2018.05.10-17
花島書店 ENSOMHEDEN

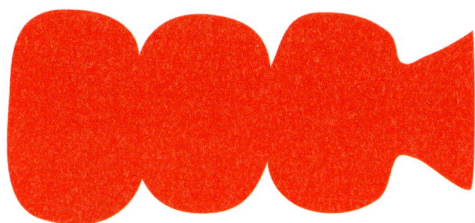

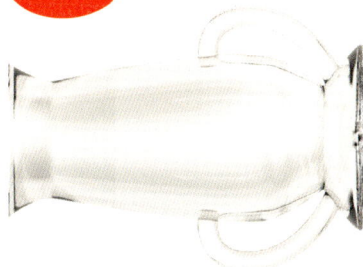

靜
物
STILL
LIFE
展

諸如事物是行其象徵意義，主要是取決於感受到這些事物的美。

TOUMEI ✕ Carolina Spencer ✕ 田井將博

時間：每日10:00-17:00 (16:30後停止售票)
詳細活動資訊：https://en.cksmh.gov/

886-2-2343-1100

Hunting Tao (Jakten på Tao)

This is a cover design for Ulrik Hegers's book about Taoism, 'Jakten på Tao' (Hunting Tao). As the theme is rather abstract, the designer decided to go with bold shapes and colors, allowing the cover to be open for interpretation.

Designer Johanne Lian Olsen | Client Ulrik Heger

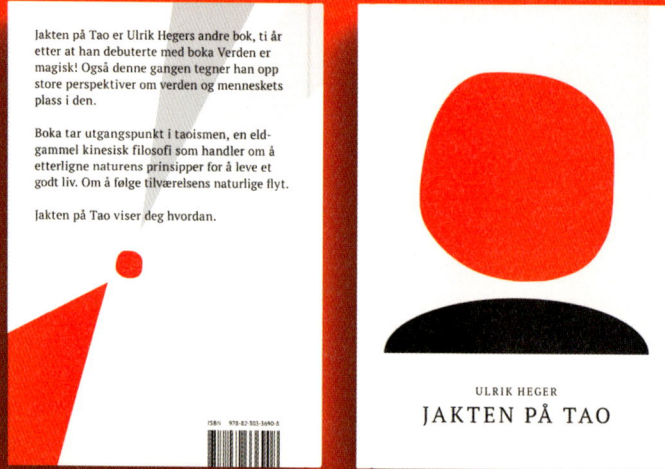

Jakten på Tao er Ulrik Hegers andre bok, ti år etter at han debuterte med boka Verden er magisk! Også denne gangen tegner han opp store perspektiver om verden og menneskets plass i den.

Boka tar utgangspunkt i taoismen, en eld-gammel kinesisk filosofi som handler om å etterligne naturens prinsipper for å leve et godt liv. Om å følge tilværelsens naturlige flyt.

Jakten på Tao viser deg hvordan.

ULRIK HEGER
JAKTEN PÅ TAO

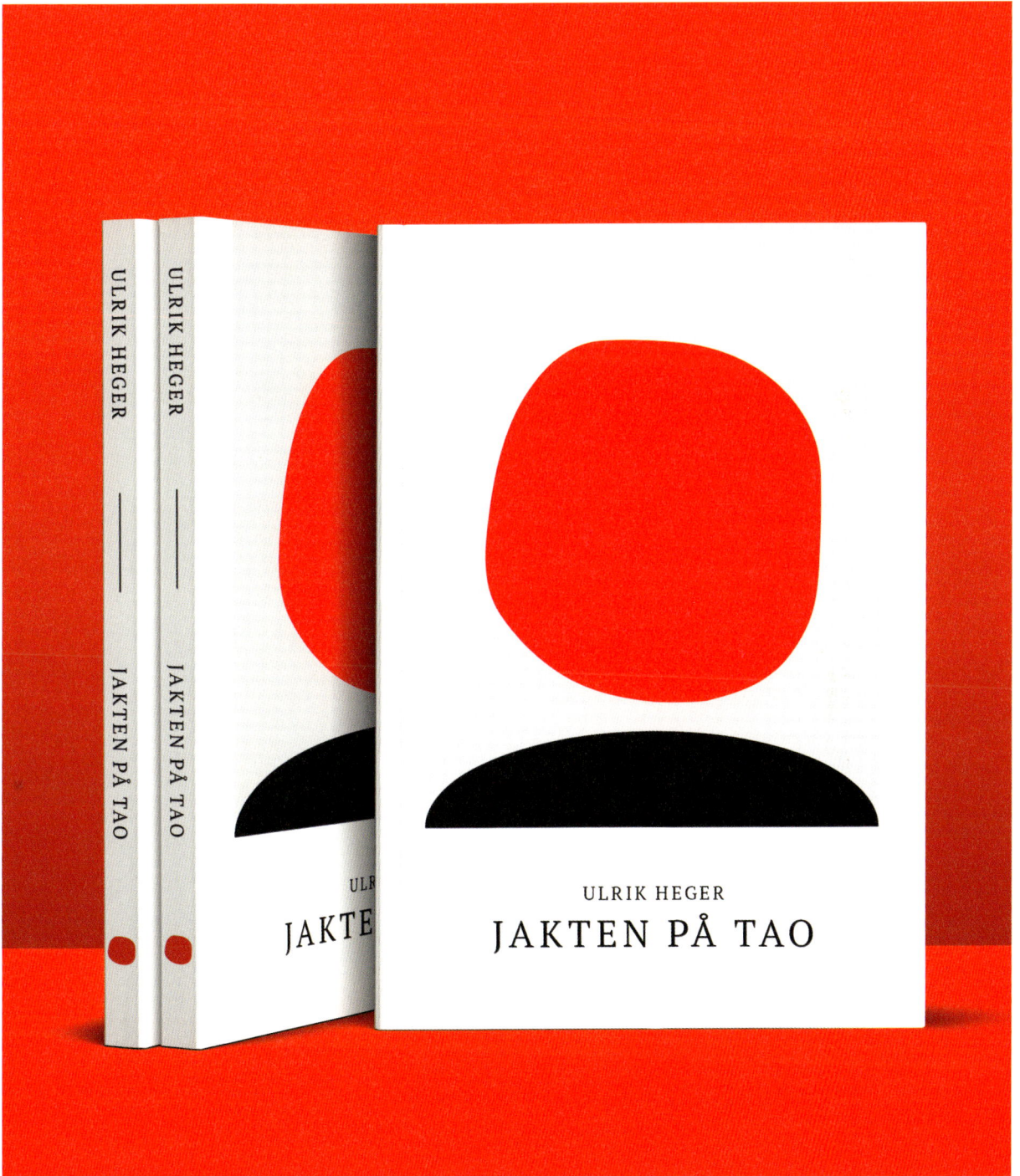

BECOMING IS MORE IMPORTANT THAN BEING.

— PAUL KLEE

BECOMING

OMA
RESID
. CO

OMA

This is a branding project for OMA, a housing project in Mexico City. The studio was inspired by the architectural style of Luis Barragán in the 1950s staring shadow-play, geometry, nature and bright colors. The logotype works with the idea of shadows and geometry. The illustrations, made merely of color blocks, portray some architectural details of the house where OMA is located.

Designer Mariela Mezquita | Client OMA

Shape of Me

The project is a very simple geometric pattern, inspired by the shapes of the new art deco style and Arabic mosaic tiles. The designer wanted to use a very basic and minimalistic form in a creative and dynamic composition with an energetic and modern color palette. She believes geometric elements are very common, so they can be applied to basically every design. There are always hundred ways to stay creative about it and create it in your own style.

Designer Monika Olbrycht

German Haus

For the "German Haus", Rocket & Wink created a new corporate design. The Bauhaus inspired design does not only find its place in the brochure "Wunderbar", but also on banners, flyers, menu cards, adverts, posters and the timetables for German band performances.

^{Designer} Dr. Rocketson & Mr. Wink | ^{Studio} Rocket & Wink | ^{Client} German Haus

MONDAY, MARCH 10
TUESDAY, MARCH 11
WEDNESDAY, MARCH 12
THURSDAY, MARCH 13
Berlin Hangover Breakfast with Axel Springer Media Entrepreneurs
German Hangover Breakfast
REEPERBAHN HAMBURGERS Interactive Edition
REEPERBAHN HAMBURGERS Music Edition
Startup pitch
Berlin Startup Corner (Elevator Pitches)
Meet the Berliners! Networking with drinks & snacks.
Hacks on Stage
WUNDERBAR An Exclusive Lunch With The Germans
Reeperbahn Festival Showcase
Berlin Music Week Drinks
Berlin Music Week Showcase
KEY:
Panel
Pitch Event
Networking Event
Showcase
Party
GERMANY AT SXSW 2014
WUNDERBAR
FEATURING
CLAIRE
MIGHTY OAKS
ROOSEVELT
INCL. GERMAN MUSIC SAMPLER
FIND OUT EVERYTHING ABOUT THE GERMAN EXHIBITORS, BANDS & EVENTS INSIDE
made in Germany
GERMAN HAUS
WUNDERBAR
AN EXCLUSIVE LUNCH WITH THE GERMANS
THURSDAY MARCH 13TH, 2014
NOON – 5 PM
GERMAN HAUS – LUCILLE
77 RAINEY STREET, AUSTIN, TX
MENU
CLAIRE, MIGHTY OAKS
ROOSEVELT

T H E   E X HIBITORS

Germany

1 FIND INFORMATION ON ALL GERMAN EXHIBITORS

HELLO AGAIN!

SXSW 2014: THANK YOU FOR HAVING US. THE GERMAN CREATIVE INDUSTRY ADORES SXSW, AND THIS YEAR IT IS REPRESENTED BY 99 CONTRIBUTORS FROM THE MUSIC, FILM AND INTERACTIVE SECTORS, AS WELL AS 17 BANDS, MAKING THIS THE BIGGEST SXSW-DELEGATION YET.

After last year's successful premiere, this year the "German Haus" will open for five days. The jam-packed itinerary reflects the range of the constantly and actively evolving German creative industry, which holds its ground not only on the home turf, but also internationally. The creative industry is an important growth sector for Germany. Despite its relative youth, it already employs 1.7 million people – one sixth of employees in this sector in the European Union. The current sales volume generated by the 244,000 German businesses amounts to more than 140 bn Euros – and counting. Startups springing from the cultural and creative sector are proof that Germany is a land of ideas and exports. With their innovative business models and ideas, startups are becoming increasingly relevant while creating necessary jobs. This year marks the first time the German Startup Association travels to Austin as part of the German delegation, to lend a voice to the German startups.

MUSIC

WUNDERBAR PRESENTS PERFORMANCES BY

DJ SETS

BALLET SCHOOL

BALLETSCHOOLBAND.COM

AROMA PITCH

WWW.AROMAPITCH.COM

ROOSEVELT

WWW.FACEBOOK.COM/
IAMROOSEVELT

TENSNAKE

TENSNAKE.
TUMBLR.COM

PLEASE REGISTER AT:
WWW.WUNDERBAR.EVENTBRITE.COM

MENU

STARTERS

"BROTZEIT" – GERMAN BREAD WITH LARD, CREAM CHEESE SPREAD WITH BELL PEPPERS AND SALTED BUTTER / CHILLED CUCUMBER SOUP WITH YOGURT / BRANDENBURG-STYLE DELI MEAT SALAD

ENTRÉE

BRAISED OX MEAT WITH HORSERADISH CREAM SAUCE / JELLIED PARSLEY HAM TERRINE / STUFFED BELL PEPPERS / MIXED ROOT VEGETABLES WITH HERB SAUCE / RUSTIC MASHED POTATOES WITH ROASTED ONIONS AND PARSLEY / MIXED GREEN VEGETABLES

DESSERT

VANILLA PUDDING WITH BLACK FOREST CHERRIES SERVED IN A JAR / GERMAN "PFLAUMENKUCHEN" PLUM SHEET CAKE WITH CINNAMON WHIPPED CREAM

Geometry Now !

R – Z

COLOGNE

RUNGE.TV

Runge.tv is an experienced full-service provider with strong competence in the area of movie and TV movie productions. In cooperation with the client, runge.tv creates an individual concept and realizes the entire production process including the areas of camera, lighting and sound management, post-production including sound recording or dubbing, graphics and quality control. It is the objective of every production that the project is comprehended in the right way, the best teams are used for the production, all opportunities of a professional post-production are utilized, and thus the best possible result is achieved for a certain movie theme. runge.tv today employs more than forty people and hast two business locations in Germany, one in Berlin and one in Cologne.

RUNGE.TV
WIDDERSDORFERSTR. 190
50858 COLOGNE
P. +49 (0)221 499 8110
F. +49 (0)221 499 8120
INFO@RUNGE.TV
WWW.RUNGE.TV

RUDOLF RUNGE
INFO@RUNGE.TV

DUESSELDORF

STATE CHANCELLERY NORTH RHINE-WESTPHALIA

NRW is Germany's media, communication and creativity hub. With some 18 million residents, it is not only the most populous state in the nation, but also an economic giant amongst Europe's regions - thanks in large measure to the media and communications industry. Following dynamic growth, the communications and media sector in NRW has for years now been among the frontrunners in the state's regional economic structures. Variety and diversity is what make the state its economy so strong. With 25,000 media and communications firms, which employ 425,000 and generate a turnover of 125 billion euros, it has evolved as the Number One centre of the media and creative industries in Germany, and as one of the leaders in Europe.

STATE
CHANCELLERY
NORTH RHINE-WESTPHALIA
STADTTOR 1
410219 DUESSELDORF
P. +49 (0)211 837 15 13
F. +49 (0)211 187 11 73
MARC.JAN.EUMANN@STK.NRW.DE
WWW.MBEM.NRW.DE

STATE SECRETARY
DR. MARC JAN EUMANN
MARC.JAN.EUMANN@STK.NRW.DE

COLOGNE

TURTLE ENTERTAINMENT GMBH

Turtle Entertainment is the world's largest eSports company leading the industry in raising eSport production and audience levels to those of mainstream sports. With offices in countries all around the world, it has a true global footprint. Turtle Entertainment creates products that cover the entire eSports spectrum. This includes high profile international tournaments such as the Intel Extreme Masters, ESL Major Series as well as grassroots amateur cups, leagues and matchmaking systems. With nearly 1 million attendees in its last Intel Extreme Masters season and tens of millions more watching at home it has been increasingly successful in its ambition to deliver amazing gaming experiences.

TURTLE ENTERTAINMENT GMBH
SIEGBURGER STR. 189
50679 COLOGNE
P. +49 (0)221 880 449 233
F. +49 (0)221 880 449 699
INFO@TURTLE-ENTERTAINMENT.COM
WWW.TURTLE-ENTERTAINMENT.COM

ULRICH SCHULZE
US@TURTLE-ENTERTAINMENT.COM

COLOGNE

UFA LAB

UFA LAB is a Berlin/Cologne based digital media content laboratory and a platform for the digital entertainment industry. Interdisciplinary teams create new transmedia concepts with a strong focus on cross-platform storytelling. They develop new content, concepts and business models for digital media and innovative online- and mobile-video products such as interactive player solutions, 2nd screen and t-commerce applications. UFA Lab is the digital production unit of UFA Film & TV Produktion, Germany's market leader in program creation, and part of FremantleMedia's international production network.

UFA LAB
SIEGBURGER STR. 215
50670 COLOGNE
P. +49 (0)221 9955 1941
INFO@UFA-LAB.COM
WWW.UFA-LAB.COM

CLAUDIA PELZER
CLAUDIA.PELZER@UFA-LAB.COM

L – R

LUENEBURG

LEUPHANA UNIVERSITY, MUSIC DEPARTMENT

Leuphana University of Lueneburg is an innovative and dynamic university focusing on the central challenges of civil society in the 21st century. In faculties focusing on sustainability research, humanities, education and management and entrepreneurship and in transdisciplinary research fields like democracy, digital Media and health, students and researchers alike have the freedom and the opportunity to broaden their field of expertise by teaming up with peers from different academic disciplines, cultures and and work environments. At Leuphana, education is understood to include the acquisition of knowledge and the skills to transform this knowledge into action for the benefit of society.

LEUPHANA UNIVERSITY,
MUSIC DEPARTMENT
SCHARNHORSTSTR. 1
21335 LUENEBURG
P. +49 (0)4131 677 2582
F. +49 (0)4131 677 2599
SCHORMANN@LEUPHANA.DE
WWW.LEUPHANA.DE

PROF. DR. CAROLA SCHORMANN
SCHORMANN@LEUPHANA.DE

DRESDEN

LOVOO GMBH

LOVOO is the number one social discovery network with a unique flirt factor. With LOVOO, users get to know people from their immediate environment. The live radar makes it possible to connect with other users anywhere at anytime. Users can chat and stay connected directly through the app. The various functions are easy to use and have an intuitive layout – perfect pre-requisites for an unforgettable flirt experience.

LOVOO GMBH
PRAGER STR. 10
01069 DRESDEN
P. +49 (0)351 418 899 42
F. +49 (0)351 418 899 38
BENJAMIN@LOVOO.COM
INSIDE.LOVOO.NET

BENJAMIN BAK
BENJAMIN@LOVOO.COM

OFFENBACH

TEXTBÜRO RAULF

Journalist, freelancer, reporter. Stefan Raulf knows how to think and write about popcultural outputs and phenomenons. For many years he monitors especially the popmusic scene. He never lost his lively interest in new topics, in new sounds, in new artists. Born in the Sixties, he still is keen to balance the passion as a fan and the knowledge as an expert. The German journalist, who studied musicology, literature and sociology, writes articles, concert reviews, hosts a radio show in Germany's Frankfurt am Main and does editorial and proofreading jobs for a publishing company.

TEXTBÜRO RAULF
AUGUST-HECHT-STR. 38
63067 OFFENBACH
P. +49 (0)179 2199 907
RAULF.TEXTE@GMX.NET
WWW.RADIOX.DE

STEFAN RAULF
RAULF.TEXTE@GMX.NET

GRÜNWALD

RTL2 FERNSEHEN GMBH & CO. KG

RTL II has been on air since 1993. The TV advertising marketing agency EL CARTEL MEDIA is a 100%-owned subsidiary of RTL II. At RTL II docusoaps show real life up close and in the flesh. Successful daily soaps inspire viewers across media boundaries. Handpicked top series along with huge cinema blockbusters thrill audiences as well. Top-notch reports and magazines offer an exciting array of fascinating topics. On top of it all, the station attracts audiences with an innovative, successful news programme concept. In 2012 RTL II attained a market share of 6.4% among 14 to 49-year-olds, turning in its best audience share for a year since 2005.

RTL2 FERNSEHEN
GMBH & CO. KG
LIL-DAGOVER-RING 1
82031 GRÜNWALD
P. +49 (0)89 641 85 0
F. +49(0) 89 64 185 9999
PRESSELOUNGE@RTL2.DE
WWW.RTL2.DE

SEBASTIAN DOPPSTADT
SEBASTIAN.DOPPSTADT@RTL2.DE

THE CIRCLE IS THE SYNTHESIS OF THE GREATEST OPPOSITIONS. IT COMBINES THE CONCENTRIC AND THE ECCENTRIC IN A SINGLE FORM AND IN EQUILIBRIUM. OF THE THREE PRIMARY FORMS, IT POINTS MOST CLEARLY TO THE FOURTH DIMENSION. — WASSILY KANDINSKY

CIRCLE

CULTURAL STRATEGY

DEBRECEN
2023. •••●
EUROPEAN CAPITAL
OF CULTURE

CANDIDATE CITY

Q/02

DOES YOUR CITY PLAN TO
INVOLVE ITS SURROUNDIN...
EXPLAIN THIS CHOICE.

The host of this bid is emphatically the city of Deb...
However, our programme shares activities both w...
immediate surroundings and the wider region, in...
cities in north-east Hungary and cross-border...
tion with cities in four countries. (This cross-b...
cooperation network is linked to the existing C...
Euroregion and hence subject of **Q09**.)

Building regional partnerships through the Ejj...
line with the long-term plans of the city to...
regional centre role within eastern Hunga...
economy, education, health services, tra...
and culture) and its (cross-border) **regio...
work-building role. In the cultural secto...
are equally supported by the city cultu...
development of festivals, the role of...
ECoC programme (projects for, in, an...

NEIGHBOURHOOD...
RESPONSIBLE CITY

Debrecen's role as a regional ce...
originating from its economic,...
responsibility for the region.

Hence, project-based coope...
and communities within a re...
an important role in the pre...
them to respond to a varie...

In terms of ecolog...
ty, Debrecen feels...
Hortobágy Natio...
site famous for it...
and low e-light...
gramme, a com...
for the Hortob...
P. 32) will star...
sustainability...
partners fro...

03

WHAT WE...

Our programm...
local values...
significance...
of Europe...
for its reg...
visions fo...
interacti...
today's t...
of an a...
Sustai...
issue...
is co...
fut...

W...

Q/01

WHY DOES YOUR CITY WISH TO TAKE PART
IN THE COMPETITION FOR THE TITLE OF
EUROPEAN CAPITAL OF CULTURE?

...ifferent ...ngos,
02. The dynamic development of the city is still an
isolated phenomenon - the direct surroundings
of the city benefit little from the growth. In the
...e region of Debrecen a significant part of the
...in deep poverty.

Debrecen 2023 — European Capital of Culture

This is the identity renewal and evolution for Debrecen 2023 European Capital of Culture. Working with the new tagline "Sharing Horizons", a new approach was taken, where the main idea of magnetic attraction is evolved further with the introduction of horizontally split layouts. As the arrows transform into to circles, abstract representations of people, ideas, and community are all drawn on to the horizon, sharing the same space and aspirations.

Studio Classmate Studio | Client EKF Debrecen 2023

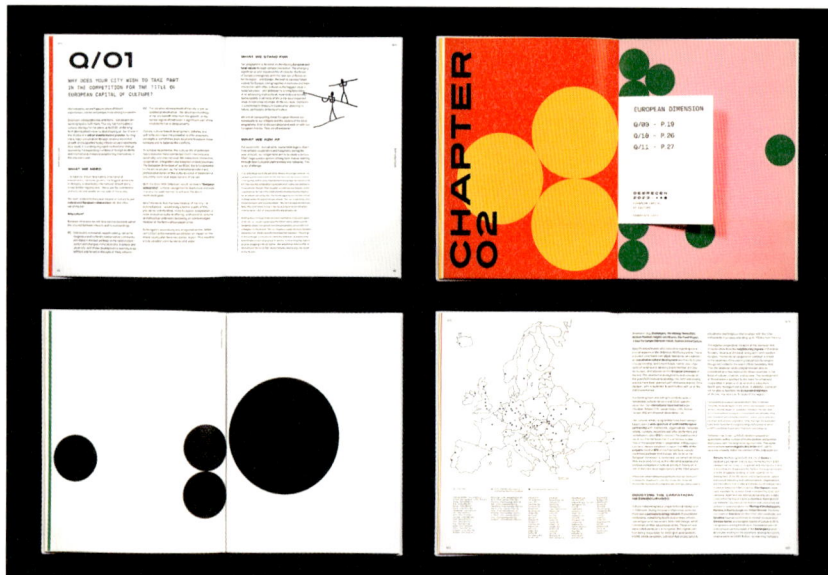

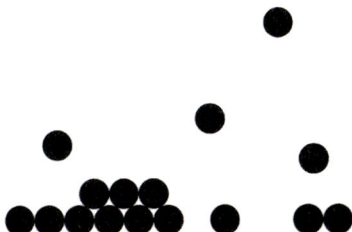

DEBRECEN
2023 · ● ● ●
EURÓPA KULTURÁLIS
FŐVÁROSA

DR. SÜLI ANDRÁS
Creative advisor

+36 30 000 000
dr.suli.andras@debrecen2023.hu
4024 Debrecen, Simonffy u. 2/A

DEBRECEN
2023 · ● ● ●
EURÓPA KULTURÁLIS
FŐVÁROSA

4024 Debrecen, Simonffy u. 2/A

DEBRECEN
2023 · ● ● ●
EURÓPA KULTURÁLIS
FŐVÁROSA

SOMOGYI-TÓTH DÁNIEL
Ügyvezető

+36 30 000 000
somogyi-toth.daniel@debrecen2023.hu
4024 Debrecen, Simonffy u. 2/A

...ble and loveable Debrecen in
...e intensive economic development and the
...hift in culture generated by the ECoC title are balanced
and complement each other for a brighter future.

PHASES	ACTIVITIES	DEBRECEN ECOC 2023	2019	2020	2021	2022	2023	2024	2025
Situation assessment (elaboration of initial data values)	exploratory representative citizen survey								
	exploratory focus group and individual interviews with representatives of the science sector								
	national image survey (media survey)								
Involvement (analyses surveys)	exploratory focus group and individual interviews with representatives of the cultural sector								
	local image survey (community life and values of local people)								
	data analyses (survey, focus group interviews, individual interviews)								
	publication of the results of data analyses, dissemination								
	elaboration and testing of event monitoring								
Implementation (event year)	social media content analysis								
	media survey								
	event monitoring								
	programme-specific questionnaire surveys								
	periodical reports, flash reports								
	media survey								
Follow-up	social media content analysis								
	tracking representative citizen survey								
	tracking focus group and individual interviews with representatives of the science sector								
	tracking focus group and individual interviews with representatives of the cultural sector								
	tracking focus group and individual interviews with secondary school students								
	preparation of closing studies, analyses, monitoring reports								

018

CHAP
03

EUROPEAN DIMENSION

Q/09 - P.19
Q/10 - P.26
Q/11 - P.27

DEBRECEN
2023 ...
EUROPEAN CAPITAL
OF CULTURE
—
CANDIDATE CITY

DEBRECEN
2023. •••
EUROPEAN CAPITAL
OF CULTURE

CANDIDATE CITY

Q/9

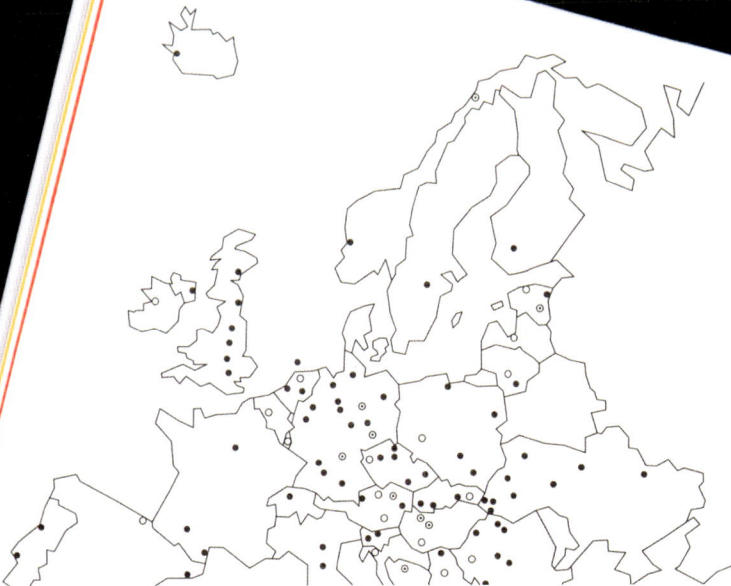

dimension (e.g. **Exchangers, The Missing,**
Horizon Festival, Heights and Mounts, The
A Soul for Europe Debrecen Forum, Scienc

Specific experts were also consulted regar
crucial aspects of the Debrecen 2023 progr
included Jordi Baltà from **UCLG,** Barcelona, w
on **sustainable cultural development** and the
city partnership, and Erhard Busek, former vic
cellor of Austria and advisory board member of
for Europe, who advised on the **European dimen**
the bid. The ceremonial arrangements and conc
the year 2023 (including opening, mid-term and c
events) have been planned with UK theatre direct
Baldwin, who is expected to work further with us o
2023 ceremonies.

Our bidding team was set up to combine wide international cultural horizons and ECoC-specific
expertise. Our **international team me**
Christian Potiron (FR), Dori
Farkas (RO) and c

063

Our Meeting Is Not a Coincidence

This is a plan B poster for promoting 2019 Innovative Trip: Our Meeting Is Not a Coincidence. This is a trip where social innovators connect and share inspiration across boundaries of regions. This poster expresses in a graphical way the solidarity and growth of local social innovators through this trip.

Designer Subin Choi | Client Jayoo Silheom (자유실험)

주최/주관 전주시사회혁신센터, 자유실험 후원 행정안전부, 전주시청

우리의 만남은
우연이 아니야

장소 춘천, 서울 일대
신청기간 19.12.09 – 19.12.20
신청링크 bit.ly/변화의빠스

19.12.27 – 19.12.29

사회혁신가들이 지역의 경계를 넘어 연결되고 영감을 나누는 여행

Public Worry Project External Activities

Public Worry Project is a humanities-based public art class where citizens especially teenagers meet in various ways under the theme of their worries and form a new perspective on themselves and others. In this project, the designer created posters promoting classes on external activities. Rather than expressing concrete and direct images, the designer sought to express abstractly with circle and curves, and went with a bright and plump atmosphere.

Designer Subin Choi | Client Gongsupyo (공수표)

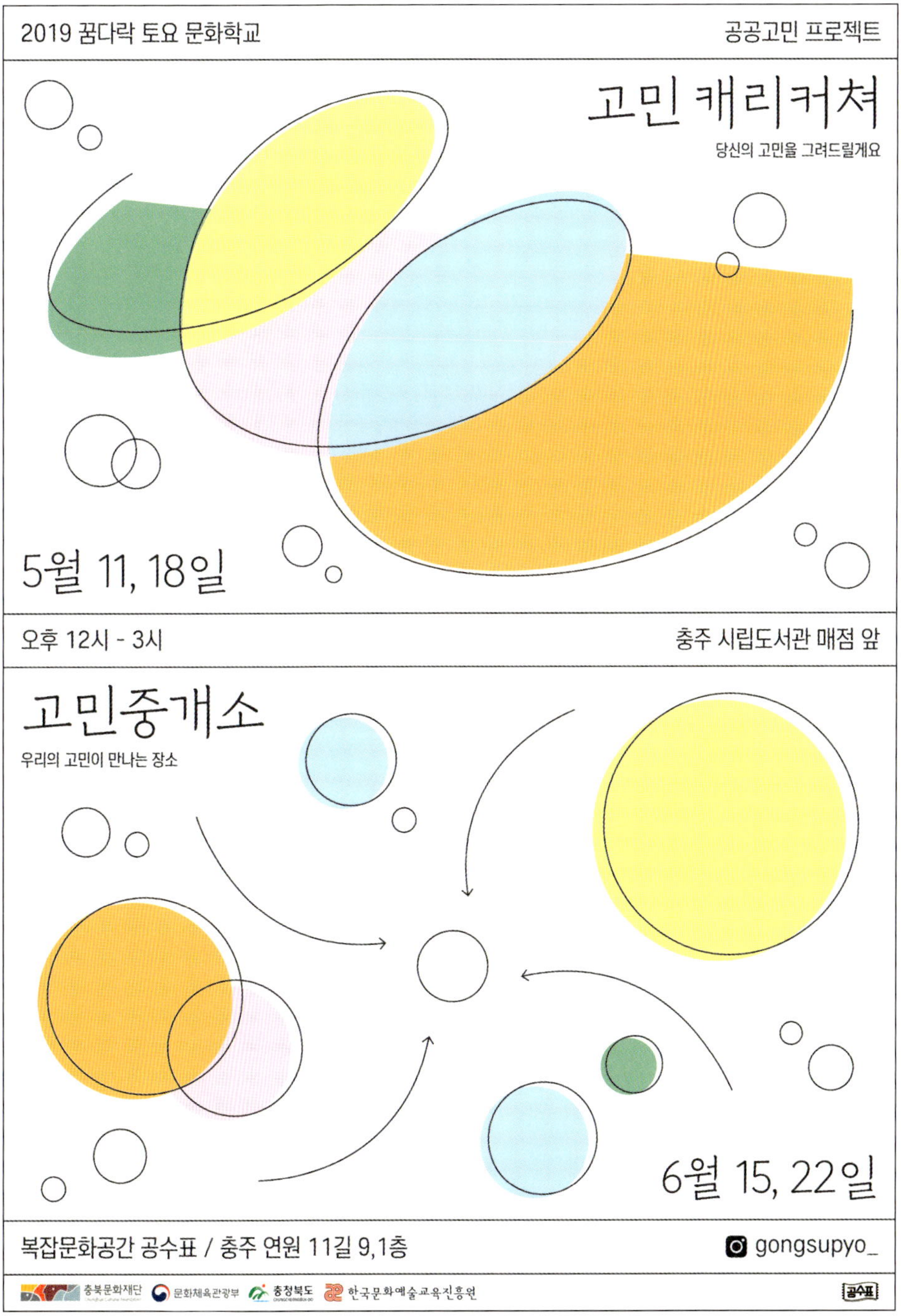

2019 꿈다락 토요 문화학교　　　　　　공공고민 프로젝트

고민 캐리커쳐
당신의 고민을 그려드릴게요

5월 11, 18일

오후 12시 - 3시　　　　　　충주 시립도서관 매점 앞

고민중개소
우리의 고민이 만나는 장소

6월 15, 22일

복잡문화공간 공수표 / 충주 연원 11길 9,1층　　　gongsupyo_

충북문화재단　문화체육관광부　충청북도　한국문화예술교육진흥원　　공수표

NetEase Kaola

The branding renewal of Netease Kaola is based on its value — Life Style Early Adopter. The studio focused on the "Kaola" (koala in Chinese) from its brand name. The logo is formed by several circles which mean a variety of products and clients. The system is diverse according to the variations of the key element, namely the circle. Through the design renewal, Netease Kaola can be consistent on various target materials.

Studio Plus X | Client NetEase

Logo Develop Process The symbol of NetEase Kaola symbolizes the significance of the that discovers and introduces value-oriented products and brands and delivers it to customers.

Various Contents

Adoption

Lifestyle Early Adopter

Primary Logo

网易考拉

Iconography Icon is a brand design element that customers can contact naturally within the service. Consistent use of icons helps customers to recognize brand attributes more easily and clearly, and builds a high quality of brand identity system.

Typography System NetEase Kaola's exclusive font, 'Ping Fang', is a neutral gothic font that has formal consistency with the refined logo type of NetEase Kaola. It is a family font that has various type so that can be applied at various touch points. It is easy to set the hierarchy of typography and has excellent readability.

Chinese

苹方-简

Chinese Typography

网易考拉,
我的生活方式。

English

PingFang

English Typography

NetEase Kaola,
Seek the
best quality.

NetEase Kaola | 02

Visual Motif System The visual motif is the most powerful brand design element that delivers the brand identity of NetEase Kaola. Using brand motif consistently shows the core value of the brand more intuitively and by expanding to various application media, we can express our stories in more effective ways.

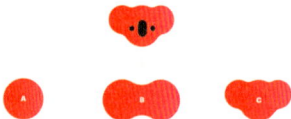

A. Circle Type A-type of circular visual motif is an initial type of symbol used by the NetEase Kaola. It can be used as a background element of various product of NetEase Kaola so that can express the variety of NetEase Kaola.

B. Connection Type B-type of visual motif can be used in combination with A-type motif, and also can be expanded to background element or frame type of variety products and models of NetEase Kaola.

C. Symbolic Type C-type of symbolic visual motif is a type that uses the symbol of NetEase Kaola as a motif, it can be used as a frame type that matches the model of NetEase Kaola. It can be applied at NetEase Kaola's various on & off-line touch points and brand promotion.

A.

B.

C.

NetEase Kaola | 03

Namecard

Envelope

Duck Tape

Id Card

Mobile App

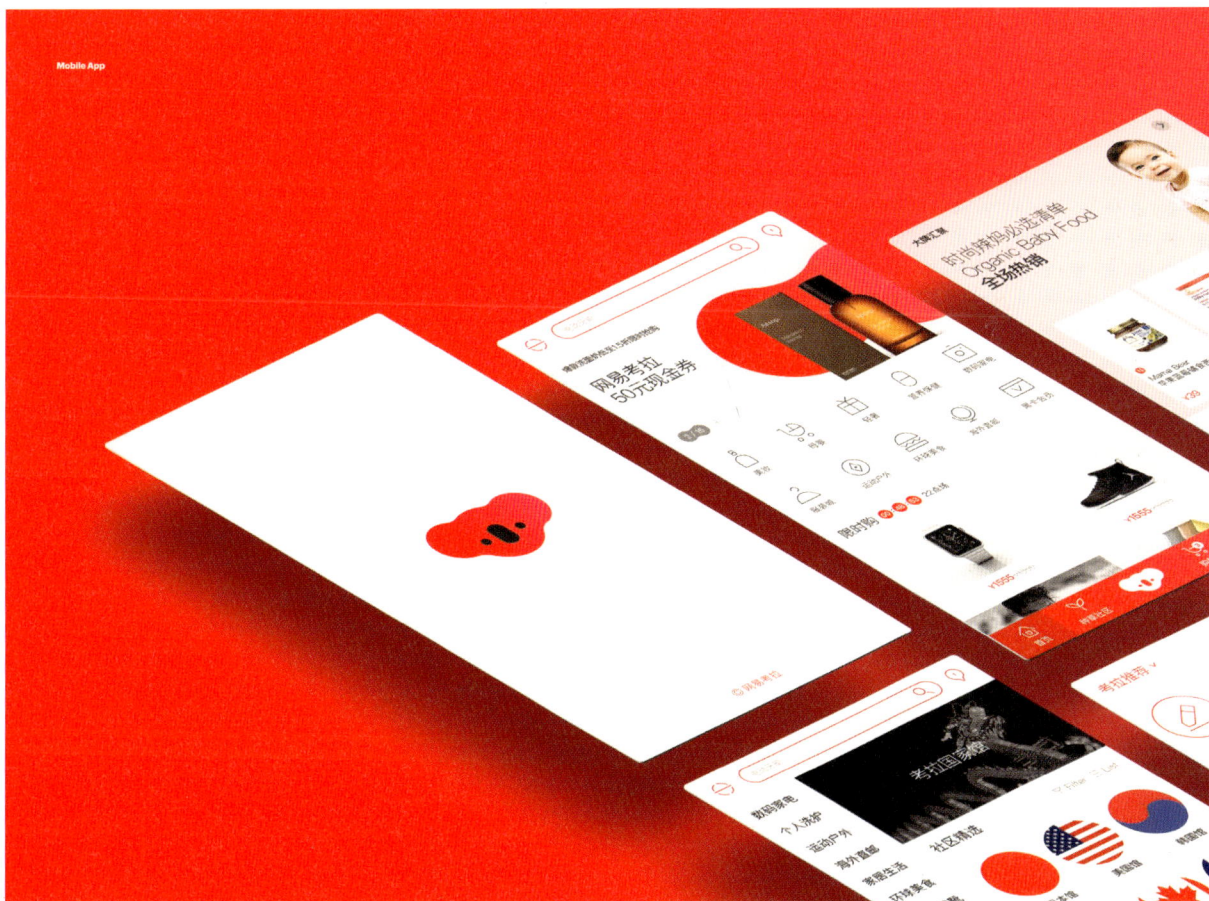

I AM AS MUCH
INTERESTED IN THE
SMALLEST DETAIL
AS IN THE WHOLE
STRUCTURE.
—MARCEL BREUER

DETAIL

Monroe Notebook

A notebook is a tool both simple and sophisticated. It is also a gift that is handy and heart-felt. An annual gift for the members of its community, The Monroe Notebook is amongst the studio's most coveted traditions. Each notebook features a unique cover design — hand painted through an array of geometric stencils. This project is a crafty way of showing that Monroe cares for its community through design.

Designer Doğukan Karapınar | Studio Monroe

Porto Shapes & Patterns

Porto Shapes and Patterns is a project born after spending over five months in Porto (Portugal). The designer made this series of posters based on tiles and patterns found through his strolls in the city which boasts thousands of beautiful patterns. The elements used in the project are among the most delicate ones. The designer, with a purpose of exploring his passion to the city and geometry, decided to pay a little tribute to not only the city itself but also how these elements of the city add to his love for geometry.

Designer Alvaro Polo Hernandez | Studio Alpoher Studio

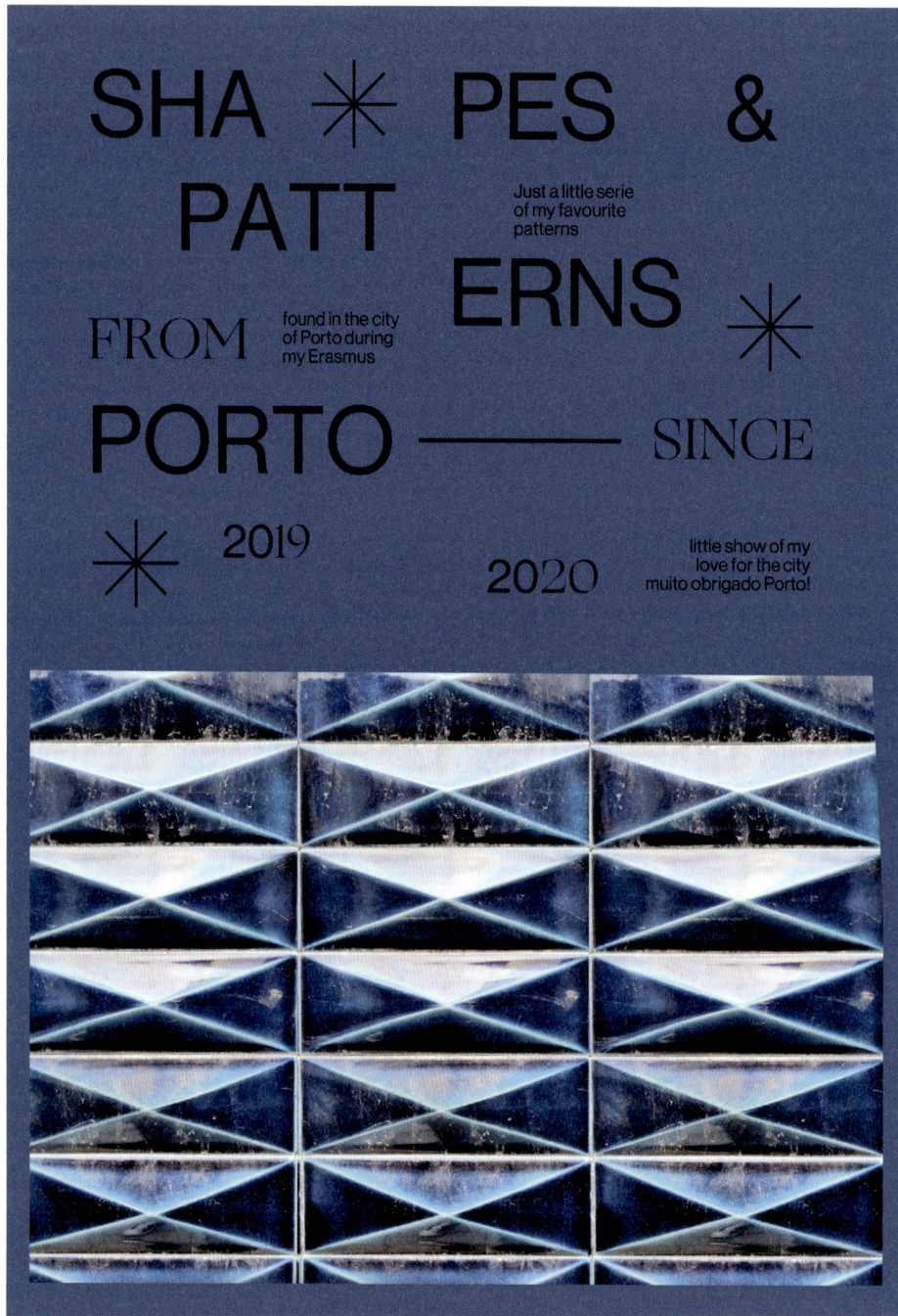

SHA ✳ PES &

PATT

Just a little serie
of my favourite
patterns

ERNS ✳

FROM   found in the city
of Porto during
my Erasmus

PORTO —————— SINCE

✳ 2019

2020   little show of my
love for the city
muito obrigado Porto!

GEOMETRIC SHAPES ARE VERY ESSENTIAL VISUAL ELEMENTS IN GRAPHIC DESIGN. COMPARED WITH ILLUSTRATIONS AND TYPEFACES, WHAT FEATURES DO YOU THINK MAKE GEOMETRIC SHAPES IRREPLACEABLE IN GRAPHIC DESIGN?

Johanne Lian Olsen

Geometric shapes are open for interpretation, and they can have numerous meanings — there is no right or wrong. Being able to play a main role in the design or lay a foundation for other content, they are super flexible. Shapes can frame images, types and others without drawing too much attention to itself, allowing you to focus on other elements like composition and balance of the design. They are not necessarily cultural or connected to certain groups in society, class etc., which makes them democratic, ageless and timeless.

Zubin Jhaveri

Geometric shapes certainly are an integral and essential part of graphic design. What sets them apart is that they are bounded by a set of rules, so you get precise outcomes when using geometry. You can simplify anything by breaking it down to its basics geometric shapes. Artists of all ages have used this method to create complex forms. Illustration and typography both are based on geometry and not the other way around. You can't make a good typeface or illustration/design without putting them under certain geometric constrains. Geometry is the very basic framework on which the most compound architectural structure can be designed. This feature has made it truly irreplaceable in all forms of design, but not just graphic design.

Xtian Miller

The versatile and multidimensional nature of geometric shapes allows a simplicity or complexity depending on the desired representation or mood. Obviously different shapes carry their own associated meanings, but when they interact with each other they can represent something entirely new, transmitting both a conscious and a subconscious message. The fundamental shapes are well established and easy to recreate, making them a useful device for quick execution, particularly in the early stages of a project. Not only can they be used in an abstract sense for the majority of commercial purposes within the field of graphic design, but also they can be applied as a framework for particular styles of art.

Monika Olbrycht

For me, the most unique feature in geometric shapes is the simplicity and universality. They usually don't have any cultural context like a gender one. They basically contain the same aesthetic value for everyone, so they can be used in any design.

Josh Harris

Geometric shapes are the building blocks of not only design but also nature and the world around us. Unlike other graphical elements, geometric shapes have been used by humans throughout history to represent and convey specific messages. Today, we can still use these basic shapes and their natural qualities to communicate messages that fail to be expressed through type or illustration. This rich history of geometric design is what makes it always such a powerful tool. Though we may see trends come and go in the using of geometry, its core philosophy and history will always be relevant in design, which brings forth timeless masterpieces.

Götz Gramlich

The simplest forms, reduced to the maximum, have always fascinated people, as they stand for perfect balance and composition. Simple as they are, they can be difficult to design with, partly because one can immediately detect every glitch and every visual imbalance in design with basic geometric shapes. But geometric shapes are of course also a remarkable visual tool to awaken the curiosity of the viewer.

Alpoher Studio

Geometry is the key element of graphic design. Everything is based on geometric shapes. If we compare it to illustration for example, you can simplify a complex illustration to elementary shapes. Besides, the individual characters of a font are a mix of different geometrical shapes put together, and such a combination of shapes makes up what we visually identify as a specific letter. With proper organizing, together they become the whole typography. Geometrical shapes are found all over graphic design without limitation in time. Graphic design to me is like what Richard Buckminster Fuller said, "Design is to make the maximum out of the minimum." And to me, geometrical shapes allow us to do that — to simplify the most out of concepts and ideas and reduce them to their minimum expression.

YOHAK DESIGN STUDIO

Illustrations can easily resonate with certain targets, but they are normally liked by a narrower range of people. The same is true of typefaces — they're great for evoking responses among people in the country the language is spoken in, but they also create a language barrier, which makes them very limited as a form of communication. On the other hand, geometric shapes are simple and straightforward, and can be easily understood by people of all ages. I think they can be a borderless, nonverbal communication tool that many people will easily accept.

Nick Barclay

I think geometric shapes are irreplaceable because they are the building blocks for everything. They can convey almost anything, and even in their simplest form, people can easily relate the shapes to the idea they are trying to convey.

Lung-Hao Chiang

Illustrations and typefaces are based on stories and plots, as well as culture. However, human appear to be born with the ability to interpret geometry intuitively regardless of the differences in culture. From the petroglyph remains of over thousands of years ago to various marks from jungles, geometric shapes are both narrative and functional, and with the passage of time, they always remain unique yet compatible with the world.

STUDIO NA.EO

In visual language, geometric shapes can communicate information directly and accurately to the audience, functioning as the handholds for designers to embody certain ideas or meanings.

Morten Kantsø

Geometric shapes are the hammers in our visual toolkit. They are powerful tools to tear down walls and nail picture frames. You could use stones, but people have evolved and nowadays we use hammers. What has been going on with the geometric shapes reflect our society.

out.o studio

We normally see geometric shapes as abstract contours of something. Different from typefaces which communicates information directly, geometric shapes can be rather simple and rational, but meanwhile, they can be figures containing a large amount of information. They always leave people a large room of imagination, which fascinates us most.

Totoro

The most distinctive features of using geometric shapes as visual elements is that they are able to cut down complexity and make things simple. The simplification from layering to flattening and from being complicated to being extremely simple enables concise and abstract elements to meet the need of the new trends.

Scandinavian Design Group

As humans, we are naturally attracted to symmetrical things. It's hard not to like geometry in design, as they are effective, easy to work with and cater for endless possibilities.

Yuka Shiramoto

Geometric patterns are simple and inorganic, but they can be expressed in various colors and shapes. There are infinite combinations, and it is possible to use them properly according to the purpose. In addition, this element goes well with any design and is easy to handle.

Gregory Page

When I first think about geometric shapes in graphic design, a lot of influences come to my mind, as well as a well-known rectangle form — used as a frame and the poster format. Geometric shapes could be defined as the basics, because the square, triangle and circle are the first one you get to know as a child. Based on mathematics, they are a standard in our world, recognizable and identifiable by everyone. Architecture, art, objects, platforms, typefaces... all these include or base on geometric shapes, and thanks to some artists, designers and movements, they have been anchored in the graphic design culture.

VERTICAL AND HORIZONTAL LINES ARE THE EXPRESSION OF TWO OPPOSING FORCES; THEY EXIST EVERYWHERE AND DOMINATE EVERYTHING; THEIR RECIPROCAL ACTION CONSTITUTES 'LIFE'. I RECOGNIZED THAT THE EQUILIBRIUM OF ANY PARTICULAR ASPECT OF NATURE RESTS ON THE EQUIVALENCE OF ITS OPPOSITES.

— PIET MONDRIAN

EQUIVALENCE

MUSEUM
OF
GUILDFORD

GUILDFORD'S
CLOCK

01.05.20
GU1 98V
£12.99

The black and gold clock has been a feature of Guildford since 1683 when the Guildhall was refurbished. According to the local council, a London clock maker named John Aylward presented the Corporation of Guildford with the projecting clock in return for the freedom to trade in the borough.

The case is made of English oak, has a cast iron internal frame and copper dials.

In this exhibition we look at what makes the landmark so spectacular, and tell its story from past to present.

The Museum of Guildford

Guildford is a town with a long history in Surrey, England. The profound history of the town is honored by the local, but for the young and new settlers, it is somewhat hard to feel the same. This project aimed to renew the branding of Guildford's Museum, hoping to help it adapt to the new age by modernizing its outdated identity system. The designer aimed at creating a dynamic branding system which would revitalize the history and the image of the town by employing bold graphic elements, with geometric shapes playing the key role in telling stories of the town's beautiful history.

Designer Josh Harris | Studio Museum of Guildford (Mock project)

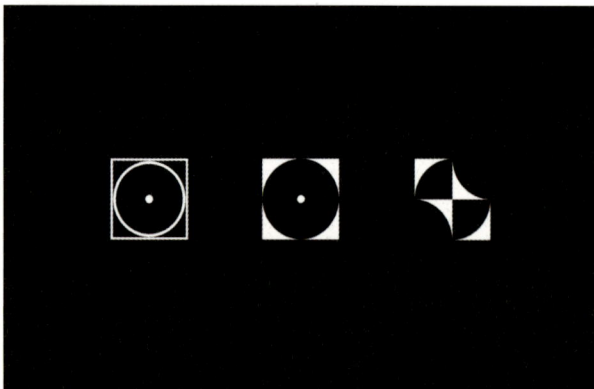

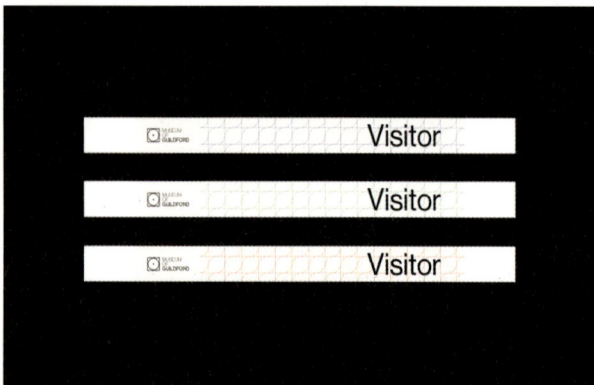

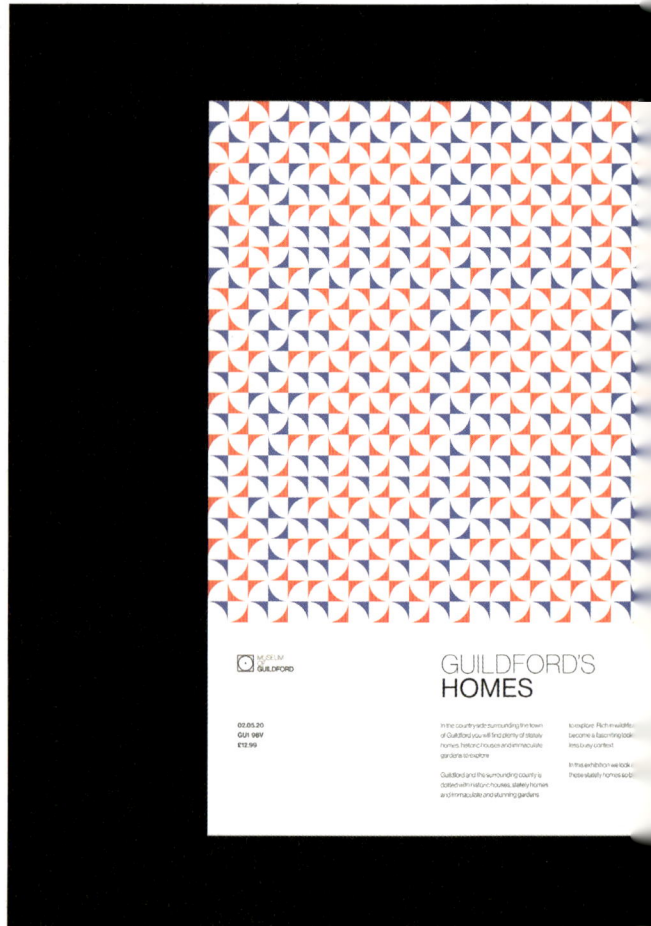

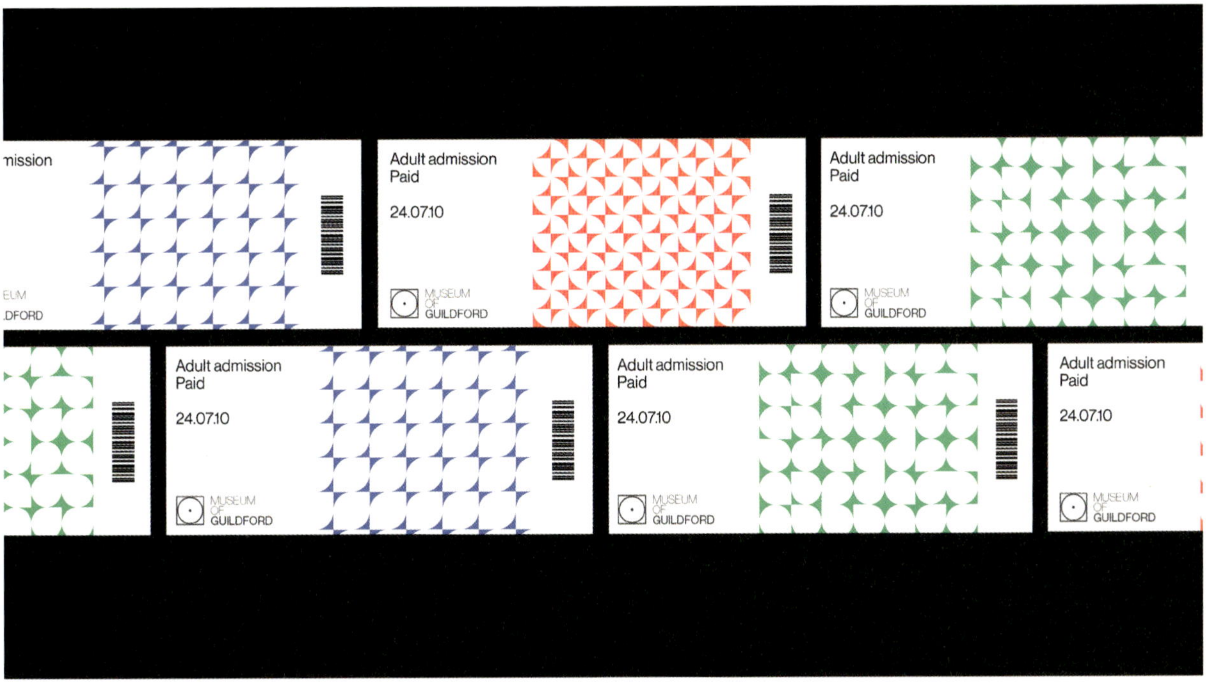

Adult admission
Paid
24.07.10

MUSEUM
OF
GUILDFORD

Adult admission
Paid
24.07.10

MUSEUM
OF
GUILDFORD

Adult admission
Paid
24.07.10

MUSEUM
OF
GUILDFORD

Adult admission
Paid
24.07.10

MUSEUM
OF
GUILDFORD

Adult admission
Paid
24.07.10

MUSEUM
OF
GUILDFORD

MUSEUM
OF
GUILDFORD

GUILDFORD'S
CLOCK

01.05.20
GU1 98V
£12.99

MUSEUM
OF
GUILDFORD

GUILDFORD'S
RIVER

03.05.20
GU1 98V
£12.99

Tudo é Tangente

"Tudo é tangente" ("Everything is tangent" in Brazilian Portuguese) was an art exhibition in Memorial Minas Gerais Vale — a cultural institution located in Belo Horizonte, southeast of Brazil. The show gathered pieces of eleven artists who worked with different poetics and platforms. In order to establish a relation with the title, the visual identity was based on the graphic vocabulary of geometry, such as mathematical statements and formal abstractions.

Designer Valquiria Rabelo | photographer Esther Azevedo | Studio Estudio Guayabo | Client Casa Camelo

TUDO É
TANGENTE

O Ministério da Cultura e a Vale apresentam
TUDO É
TANGENTE

O Ministério da Cultura e a Vale apresentam

TUDO
TANG

Geometry Now !

O Ministério da Cultura e a Vale apresentam

TUDO É
TANGENTE

Artistas
Daniel António
Daniel Pinho
David Magila
Felipe Chimicatti
Hortência Abreu

Lucas Ero
Noemi Assumpção
Olivia Viana
Pedro Carvalho
Randolpho Lamonier
Ricardo Burgarelli

TO BE ONESELF IS
BEING NEITHER UNDER
BOND NOR BORROWED
NOR SOLD NOR HIRED.
TO BE, MEANS TO BE
SPIRITUALLY FREE.
— THEO VAN DOESBURG

FREE

Pollen

Pollen is a fluid and inclusive, multi-genre Spotify playlist that champions and propels the best new music and art. The design system reflects Pollen's "hand-picked" method of compilation, which means that all contents are curated by real people instead of algorithms. Its signature element is a library of pollen-like organic shapes. The color palette is equally flexible, adapting to each artist and resulting in strange and unexpected combinations that emulate their individual moods.

Designer Felipe Rocha | Studio PORTO ROCHA | Client Spotify

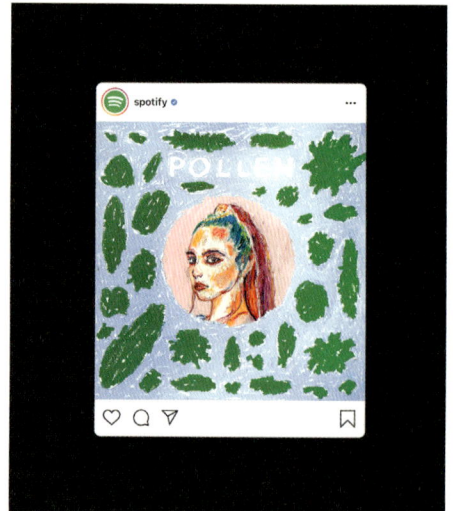

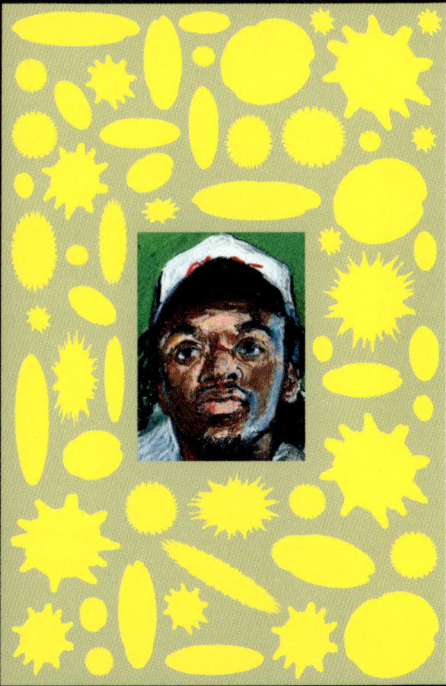

MERMAID to Umi

The designer designed a book cover, MERMAID to Umi, using a TAKEO's paper in a new color palette named Mermaid. Believing that reading a book is like floating in the ocean, in the cover design, the designer used soft curves to create an abstract ocean and put a mermaid in it. In this way, she built up a scene where the mermaid swims gracefully in the fantastic ocean of stories. The project was published in the monthly, *Brain*. A solo exhibition on the theme of the book cover was successfully held as part of the "BOOK BOX" project at DAIKANYAMA TSUTAYA BOOKS. Aiming at showcasing the quality of the paper, the exhibition space was designed as a small paper ocean.

Designer Ayaka Shimizu | Client DAIKANYAMA TSUTAYA BOOKS, Sendenkaigi Co., Ltd., *BRAIN*, TAKEO CO., LTD.

New Year's Card 2020

The designer designed a New Year's card for 2020, the year of the rat. In the card, there is a rat in an abstract geometric shape, which takes up most of the space in the card. The card was printed on TAKEO's paper, with the use of planographic printing, which allows it to feature a unique texture. The card successfully made its way to the "New Year's Card from 100 Creators" exhibition planned by TAKEO.

Designer Ayaka Shimizu

Creators Meet TAKAOKA

The designer, using gentle curves and geometric shapes, helped to deliver the visual identity and the space design for the PR event, Creators Meet TAKAOKA. The event, held in Shibuya Hikarie, was about Takaoka's craftsmanship and its secrets. It introduced new forms of manufacturing in Takaoka by highlighting the bond between the craftsmanship that has been passed down from ancient times and modern creators in Takaoka.

Designer Ayaka Shimizu | Studio NON-GRID INC. |

Client "Mizu to Takumi" Toyama West Tourism Promotion Association

Creators Meet TAKAOKA

高岡の、匠の技と秘密
地域で出合う新しいものづくりの形

2019.10.7.
@渋谷ヒカリエ8F「COURT」

Creators Meet TAKAOKA

高岡の、匠の技と秘密
地域で出合う新しいものづくりの形

日時：2019年10月7日(月)11:00〜20:30
内容：展示　ワークショップ　トークセッション・交流会　w/a 高岡市の美味しいもの by d47
会場：渋谷ヒカリエ8F「COURT」(東京都渋谷区渋谷2-21-1)

トークゲスト：ナガオカケンメイ(デザイン活動家)／小池博史(クリエイティブディレクター)／
佐野文彦(美術作家・建築家)／島有造(鋳金職人)／尾崎迅(金工作家)
伝統工芸ワークショップ講師：武蔵川剛嗣(鋳金職人)／島谷好徳(鋳金職人)

地域はクリエイターの創造性を拡張し、
クリエイターは地域のものづくりを革新する。

● 展示：11:00〜20:30

● ワークショップ：11:00〜18:00

● トークセッション・交流会：19:00〜20:30

2019.11.22〜23(1泊2日)、富山県高岡市でクリエイター向けのツアーを実施します。
伝統〜先端までものづくり工房・工場や歴史文化を訪ねる旅。本イベントにて参加者を募集します！

MODERN MAN LIVES
MORE AND MORE IN
A PREPONDERANTLY
GEOMETRIC ORDER.
ALL HUMAN CREATION
MECHANICAL
OR INDUSTRIAL
IS DEPENDENT
UPON GEOMETRIC
INTENTIONS.
— FERNAND LÉGER

GEOMETRIC

CareerTrackers
Indigenous Internship
Program

CareerTrackers Awards Cards

CareerTrackers creates paid internship opportunities for indigenous university students in Australia. These cards were created as part of the materials for their gala awards evening. The cards were used to carry the program for the evening and stacked together as a table decoration during the awards presentation dinner.

Designer Paul Garbett | Studio Studio Garbett | Client CareerTrackers

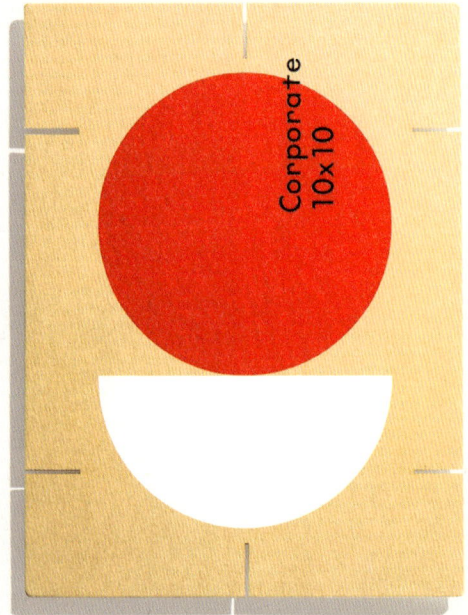

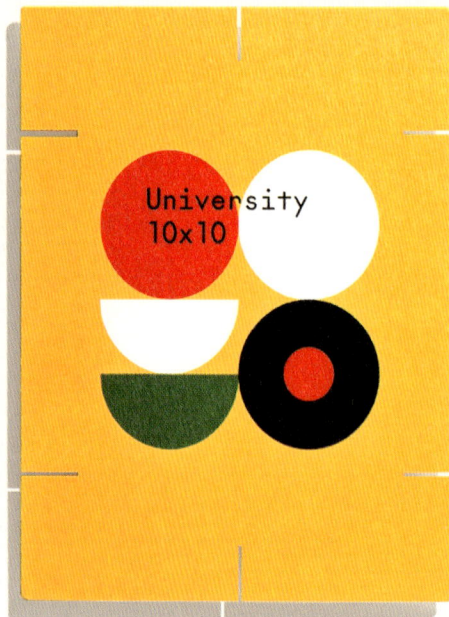

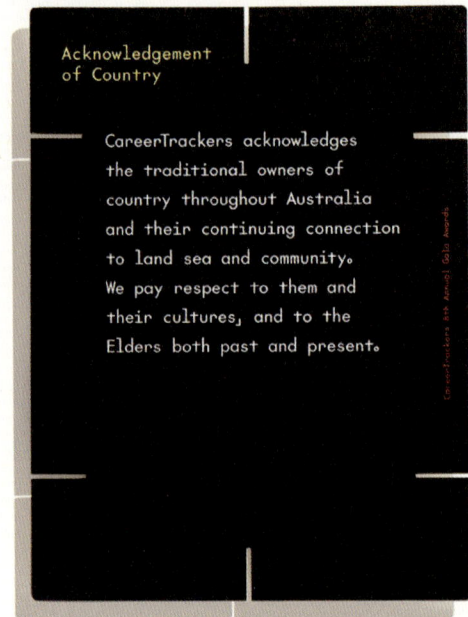

8th Annual Gala Awards

Corporate 10x10

University 10x10

Acknowledgement of Country

CareerTrackers acknowledges the traditional owners of country throughout Australia and their continuing connection to land sea and community. We pay respect to them and their cultures, and to the Elders both past and present.

CEO's

8th Annual Dinner Awards

University 10×10

CEO's Welcome

Acknowledgement of Country

CareerTrackers acknowledges the traditional owners of Country throughout Australia

Excellence Award - New in 2018!

...ni Excellence Award is given to a
... of the CareerTrackers program who is
...g in their career, promoting the overall
...f CareerTrackers and paying it forward
... a positive role model for the next
...on of Indigenous professionals. The
...xcellence Award is a new award in 2018.

CareerTrackers 8th Annual Gala Awards

UTS

2018 Partnership for Excellence

Geometry Now !

2018 CareerTrackers Interns

2018 CareerTrackers Interns

2019 SeMA HANA Art Criticism Award

The 2019 SeMA HANA Art Criticism Award is an open call for critics from all backgrounds. Applicants are then assessed entirely by their ability to critique, not by any other discriminatory factors such as age and academic backgrounds. The graphic design for the award appeals to the young spectators by the use of fun geometries and vibrant colors. By imbuing a sense of motion, the studio also tried to convey the committee's progressive vision.

Designer Hyejin Kil (graphic design), Joonho Kwon (design direction), Moa Ku (lettering)

Studio Everyday Practice | Client Seoul Museum of Art (SeMA)

SEOUL MUSEUM OF ART

서울시립미술관
SEOUL MUSEUM OF ART   하나금융그룹

2019 SeMA-하나 평론상
수상자 이진실, 장지한

12. 3. 화. 오후 2시
정동1928 아트센터 2층 이벤트홀

2019 SeMA-HANA Art Criticism Award

올해부터 수상자는 상금 2천만 원과 함께
'2020 SeMA 비평연구 프로젝트'
활동을 지원받습니다.

서울시립미술관   하나금융그룹

미래 비전의 평론을 실천할 '일

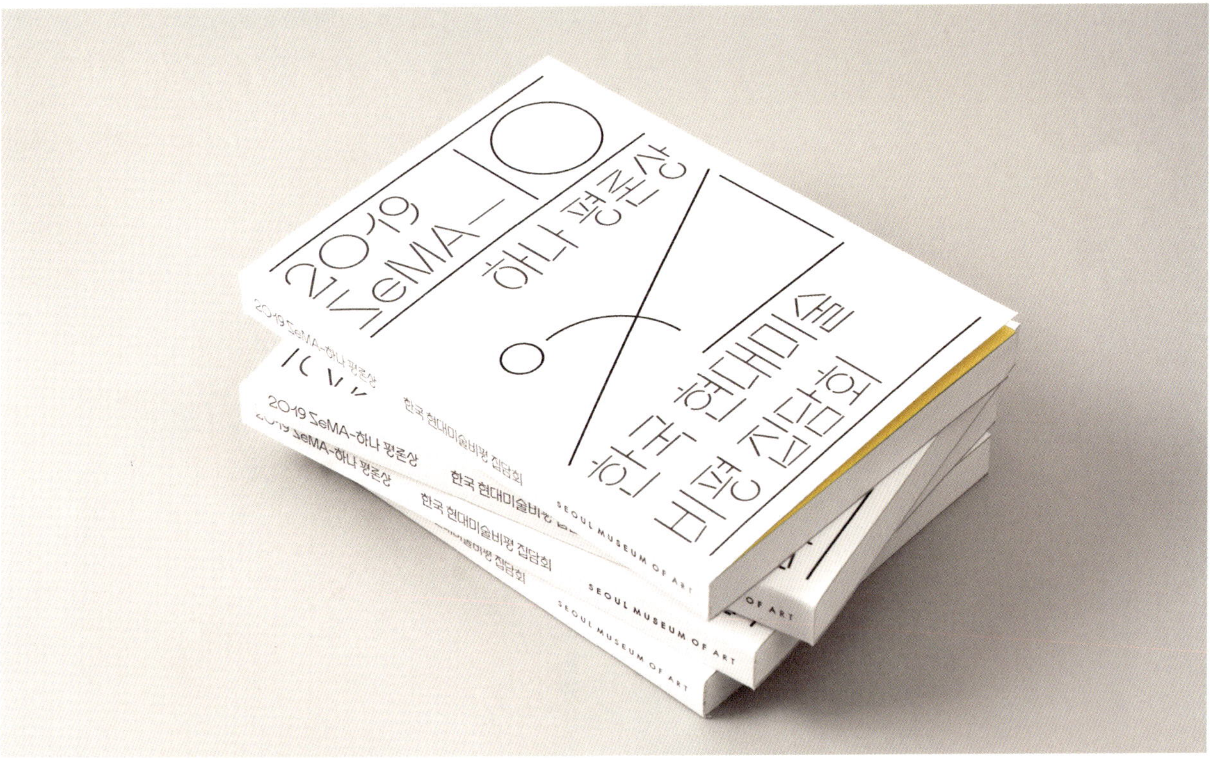

서울시립미술관(SeMA)이 한국 미술평론에
새로운 동력이 될 평론가를 찾습니다.

SEOUL
MUSEUM
OF ART

진취적인 평론   지속가능한 평론   미래 비전의 평론

하나 평론상

SEOUL
MUSEUM
OF ART

A-HANA Art Criticism

하나
평론상

2019
한국
현대미술
비평 집담회

SEOUL
MUSEUM
OF ART

비평(가)의 프로젝트
Projects of (Critical) Writers

12. 3. 화. 오후 3시–6시
정동1928 아트센터
2층 이벤트홀

곽영빈, 김정현, 남웅, 문정현
기획 및 진행: 윤원화

서울시립미술관   하나금융그룹

2019
SeMA
하나
평론상
시상식

SEOUL
MUSEUM
OF ART

2019 SeMA-HANA Art Criticism Award

2019 SeMA-
하나 평론상 수상자
이진실, 장지한

12. 3. 화. 오후 2시
정동1928 아트센터
2층 이벤트홀

서울시립미술관   하나금융그룹

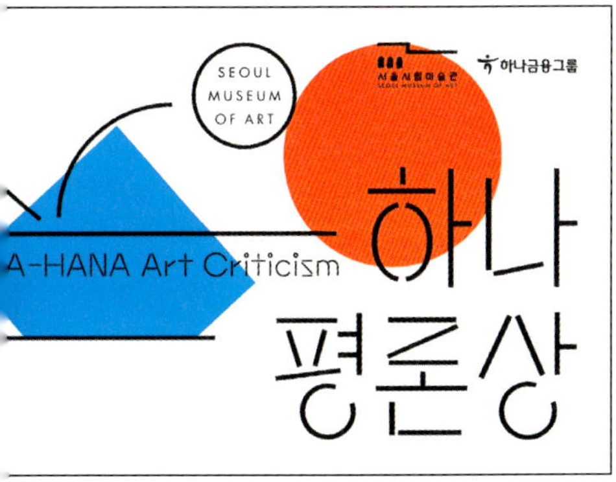

Funk Noir

This is a sleeve design for 12" sound sampler by Stockholm based house and electronica label Funk Noir. The cover using offset printing is in two colors with added sticker (same as the sticker on the vinyl record). The sleeve also uses red transparent vinyl.

Designer Håkan Ängquist | Studio Nuet Studios | Client Funk Noir

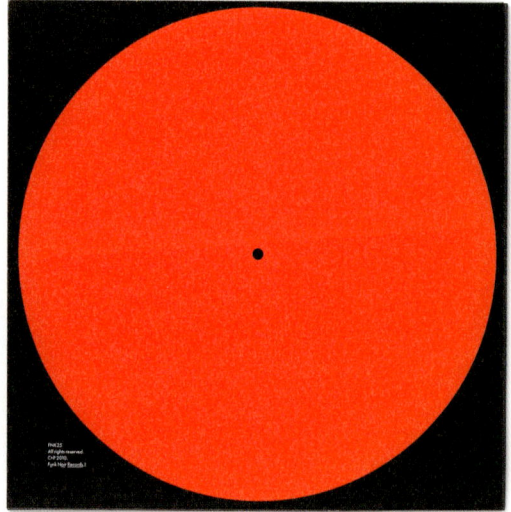

Spielzeug Typeface

"Spielzeug" Typeface was Jemima Holmes' final artwork for her graphic design course with Bauhaus Summer School in Bauhaus University, Weimar, Germany. It was inspired by the shapes and colors of the toys created by Alma Siedhoff-Buscher, a well-known Bauhaus student and designer. Jemima Holmes has created two versions of the typeface: one that follows the thick shapes of the toys, and the other with the thick shapes having been translated into thin lines. The colors for both versions are completely customizable depending on the user.

Designer Jemima Holmes

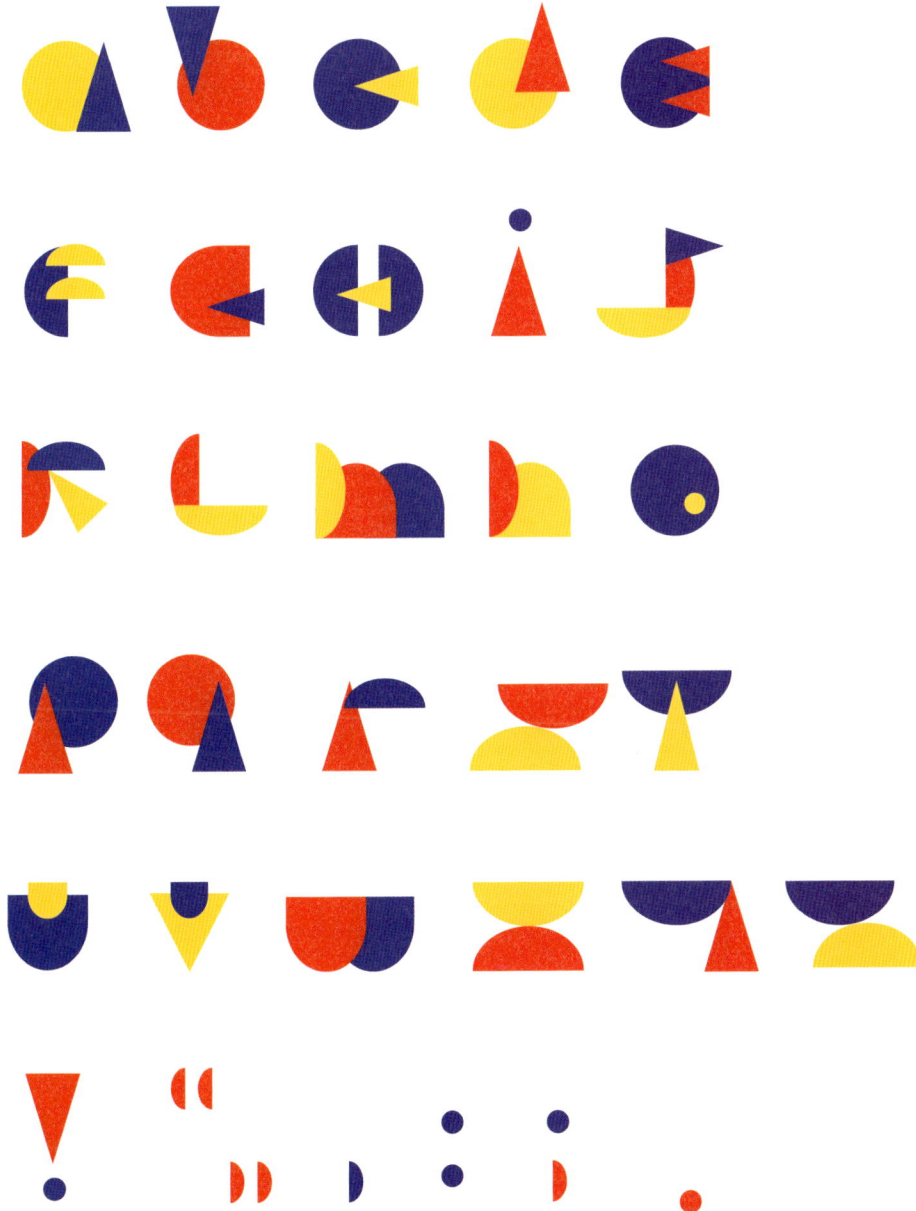

TO ACHIEVE VITAL HARMONY IN A PICTURE IT MUST BE CONSTRUCTED OUT OF PARTS IN THEMSELVES INCOMPLETE, BROUGHT INTO HARMONY ONLY AT THE LAST STROKE.
— PAUL KLEE

HARMONY

Objects

The works are like simple and clean still life, but they are telling beautiful personal stories of the artist, like stories of heart-breaking experience and stories of meeting stray cats...

Designer Seamoon

Geometry Now !

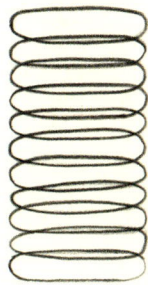

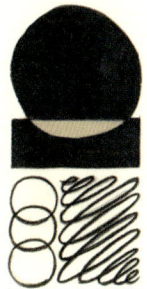

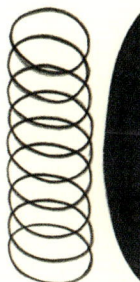
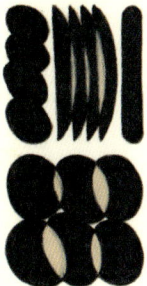

Interview

WHAT DO YOU THINK IS THE GREATEST CHARM OF EMPLOYING GEOMETRIC ELEMENTS IN VISUAL DESIGN?

Totoro

In visual language, geometric shapes make it possible to express abstract ideas with a bunch of seemingly simple elements, which leaves a huge space for the designer to create. Therefore, I believe that the greatest charm of geometric shapes is that it is able to communicate complex ideas in rather simple ways.

YOHAK DESIGN STUDIO

The greatest charm is that geometric forms are highly abstract, so they can create expressive designs that will inspire the imaginations of people who see them. They can make a design more durable and useful, since they are less connected to specific events and have fewer restrictive elements than a figurative one.

Zubin Jhaveri

To me geometry is essentially math. It is very logical and has a fixed answer. The human eye finds symmetry pleasing and you can truly mesmerize someone using the equilibrium that geometry can create. It is fascinating how applying a fixed geometric element in the right way can create the illusion of motion. It seems limiting but when you really start to play with it you can unravel the endless possibilities. It flawlessly combines both sharp edges and angles with smooth curves. The greatest charm of using these elements in visual design is that in this process, one is seeking to seemingly break the rules while yet still playing within the boundaries of geometry.

Yuka Shiramoto

I think the biggest attraction of geometric shapes is that they have a beautiful and functional design. It is also a design that many people will accept in their daily lives.

Chris Page

The greatest charm in using geometric elements in design is their versatility. The same shape can be treated differently to trigger a different emotion or purpose. Changing their color or formation can portray the feeling of being bold and playful, soft and understated or hard and purposeful.

Sakai Hiroko

Since geometric elements are simple shapes, their greatest charm is that they have various meanings depending on the imagination of the viewer.

Ayaka Shimizu

The greatest charm is that geometric shapes can leave a strong impression on viewers, because it is symbolic.

STUDIO NA.EO

They are completely independent.

Morten Kantsø

Geometric shapes are easy to use and they are very efficient in creating balance in a composition. They work without limitation to the style. The first thing you learn about design are related to geometric shapes, like Bauhaus: Kandinsky's basic design, Albers' squares. It is the default mode of the graphic designer.

Subin Choi

Since geometric elements have no specific forms, they could represent something abstract such as feelings, impressions, etc. I think this is the greatest charm of geometric elements. People can express diverse impressions or feelings by using a combination of colors and geometric elements. And also, geometric elements make viewers imagine rather than deliver the message directly. Interestingly, even if we look at the same element, the interpretation or the impression could be different depending on the person who sees the element.

Josh Harris

The endless possibilities of geometry is what seems to draw me to it so often. Exploring new possibilities through patterns and textures, and applying them to different mediums can often lead to some of my most exciting works. The application to different mediums of art and design allows geometric elements to be such a loved asset within the design community and wider audiences. Using simply one or two shapes can offer us huge opportunities within our designs. Changing simple elements of the shapes can lead us to a unique perspective which can offer new energy and depth to our works.

DO YOU THINK USING GEOMETRIC SHAPES IN GRAPHIC DESIGN WOULD BE AFFECTED BY DIFFERENT STYLES OR GENRES OF ART? WHAT ARE THE EFFECTS?

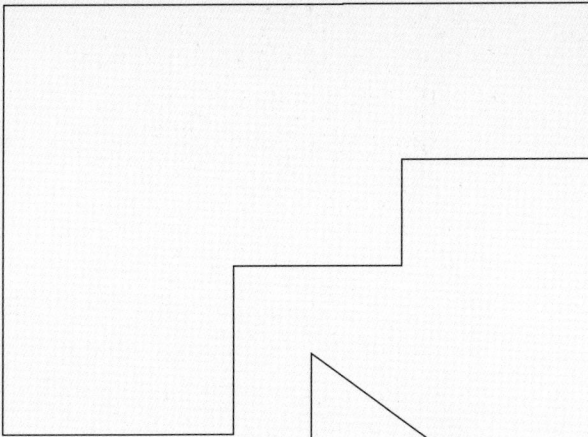

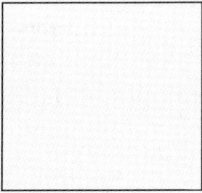

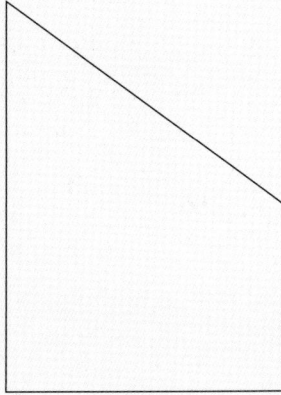

Götz Gramlich

Effects, zeitgeist style are eye-candy that hide the true beauty of the form. I prefer harmony between form and style. For example, monochrome surfaces or contours.

Lung-Hao Chiang

In different culture and different environment, shapes can be interpreted differently. Take the buttons on the gamepad as an example. In Asia, we tend to take "○" as "OK", and "×" as "cancel", but the opposite is true in Europe and America. When filling in forms, Asian people prefer "√", while European and American people tend to use "×". We can see that even the most basic geometric shapes can be interpreted differently in different culture and situations, so cultural diversity matters in design.

Ayaka Shimizu

When doing design, I am always influenced by various things, including art styles of course, as well as various products on the market, SNS, books, and so on. I think that being influenced can prevent the expression from being completed in the narrow sense of the individual.

Monika Olbrycht

Of course, it is happening all the time. For example right now we see lots of 3D geometric shapes in bright colors that are used in many animations related with digital reality. But at the same time, we see a lot of golden, linear geometric elements that are inspired by art deco style, and combined with natural structures. I would say that the effect can be whatever the artist want to achieve and that is exactly what makes geometry so universal and great.

ILLUSIONS ARE SIMPLE FACTS, BUT THEY HAVE BEEN CREATED BY THE MIND, BY THE SPIRIT, AND THEY ARE ONE OF THE JUSTIFICATIONS OF THE NEW SPATIAL CONFIGURATION. — GEORGES BRAQUE

ILLUSION

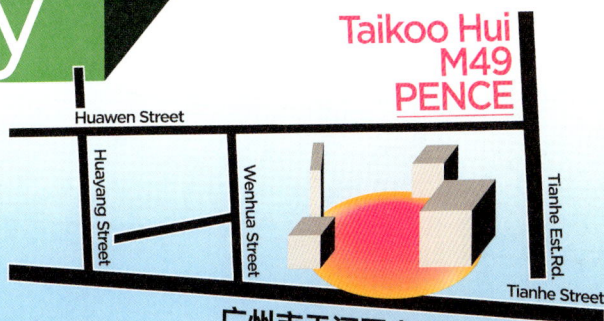

Pence

Pence is a brand with a predominantly male audience. Pence is the plurality of penny, which implies "many a little makes a mickle". The "P" from the brand name is the core of the visual identity. The fairly simple shape of the "P" , on the other hand, enables huge possibilities for its design. On this basis, the designers decided to go with circles and squares. The two elements which make up the word "P" become the foundation of the design. By constant replication and adjustment, different combinations of circles and squares eventually form the visual system. The project was nominated for the Tokyo TDC Annual Awards.

Designer Liu ZhiZhi, Mazzybox, Chen Chaohao | Studio STUDIO NA.EO | Client Pence

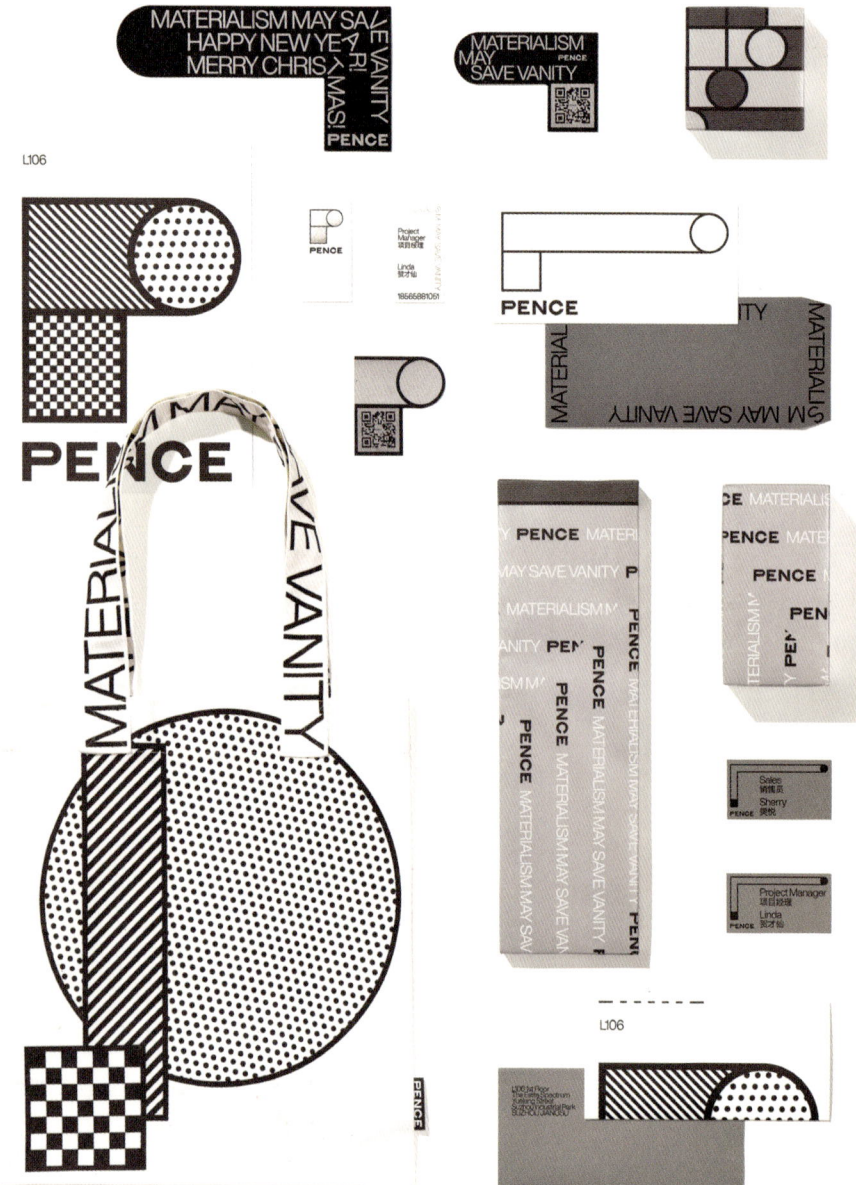

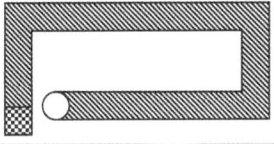

PENCE

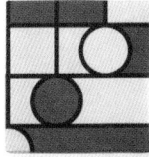

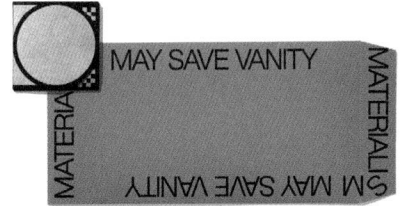

MAY SAVE VANITY

MATERIALISM MAY SAVE VANITY

PENCE

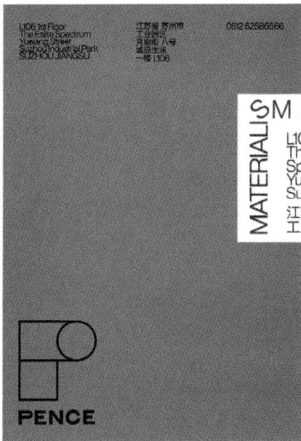

MATERIALISM MAY SAVE VANITY

L106 1st Floor
The Eslite
Spectrum
Yuelang Street
Suzhou

Industrial Park
SUZHOU
JIANGSU

051262586566

江苏省 苏州市
工业园区

月廊街 八号
诚品生活
一楼 L106

PENCE

Quarantine Posters 2020

During the quarantine time, the designer made some posters as a personal exploration to break with boredom and also give some reminders to help the cause and encourage people to stay home. The designer used some very simple sentences, geometrical shapes and special textures, with a restricted color scheme of pink, black and white, to represent his feelings and the situations.

Designer Alvaro Polo Hernandez | Studio Alpoher Studio

Self isolation   2020

40   alpoherstd

Sta
Ho
Sta
Sa

Stay
Home

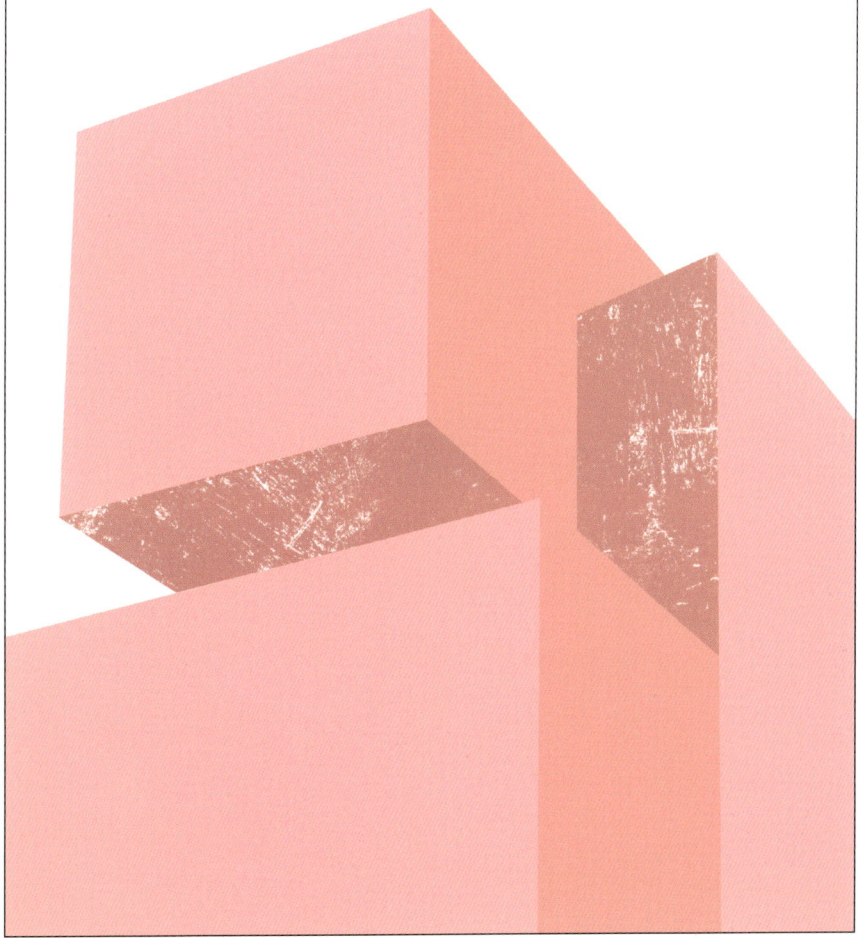

Wrapping Paper

Put down that shiny roll of wrapping paper and pick up a piece of newsprint instead. Cut paper collages were photographed and digitally composed to create a series of graphic compositions and repeats. The designs were placed onto a newspaper layout in a traditional broadsheet format, pairing patterns with compositions on the reverse. The design ended up being a collection of bold and delicately designed wrapping paper.

Designer Heidi Chisholm, Emma Sobota, Leigh Nelson | Studio LMNOP Creative

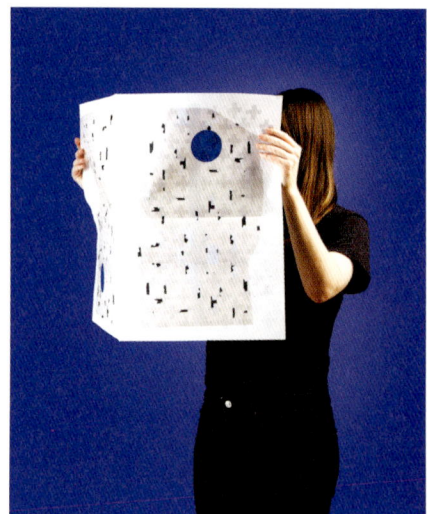

Geometry Now !

EVERYTHING EXISTS IN LIMITED QUANTITY — ESPECIALLY JOY. — PABLO PICASSO

JOY

CFT Shop & Learn

Credit For Teens is a project about teaching teens how to use credit wisely. The studio had a lot of fun making a bunch of funny combinations of shapes. The combinations were developed into a series of set designs to highlight the product. Dynamic and playful layouts using geometric shapes and strong colors — the combination represents the fun of being young.

Designer Luján Borzi, Josefina Llano, Carolina Carballo, Valeria Moreiro | Studio NOT REAL |
Client CREDIT FOR TEENS

A Pylon symbolizes the temporary nature of the project, and the artistic installations involved. Three-color silkscreen print on gray paper, using the characteristic neon color of classic traffic cones.

Designer Götz Gramlich | Studio gggrafik-design | Client Pascal Baumgaertner

Randy Weston & African Rhythms Duo

This is a poster for announcing the Jazz concert with Randy Weston & African Rhythms Duo in Willisau, Switzerlan. The idea came from the research in African patterns. It looks like textile but in a very rhythmical way.

Designer Niklaus Troxler | Studio Niklaus Troxler Design

Willisau, Freitag 22. Febr. 91

20.00 Uhr, Hotel Mohren

Randy Weston & African Rhythms Duo

feat. Eric Asante

Fathers Wine Packaging & Identity

Fathers Wine is a small family winery in Ukraine, run by the founder's children. Their main values are simplicity, sincerity and family. The studio created a system of primitive geometrical shapes inspired by traditional Ukrainian symbols to emphasize Fathers Wine's simplicity and show that it's secrets are passed down from generation to generation.

Designer Leonid Nakonechnyi | Studio R Agency | Client Fathers Wine VB

Fathers© Wine

Coat of arms generator

Background:

Father's Wine is a real family business. It's a small winery in Ukraine, founded by a man, whose children now run it. Their main values are simplicity, sincerity and family. Father's Wine core idea is not to be another fancy drink, but a good basic wine for everyday.

Execution:

We divided our work in 2 phases: graphic design and coat of arms generator.

First, to emphasize that Father's wine is a good basic wine which secrets are passed down from generation to generation, we created a system of simple geometrical shapes inspired by traditional Ukrainian symbols and filled the whole bottle with it.

Problem:

Create a packaging design for a new wine series of a brand that doesn't want to be another 'look I'm so heritage' guy and wants to promote family values.

Then on the back of the bottle we created a field in the shape of a heraldic shield. It's a canvas for creating your own family coat of arms with a set of stickers that are distributed with every bottle. Those stickers are the same geometrical shapes that we created for our packing design. Families can combine them, give them their own meanings or just have fun.

Idea:

Create a system of simple geometrical shapes inspired by traditional Ukrainian symbolics to emphasize that Fathers Wine is a good basic wine which secrets are passed down from generation to generation.

Results:

After the launch we got **40000** media impressions without any investment.

ART MAKES
SOMETHING A LOT
MORE KENSPECKLE OR
AUDIBLE.
— PAUL KLEE

KENSPECKLE

Raining Coffee

Raining coffee is an independent coffee brand. Only after having undergone the rainy days can the coffee beans become truly mature. The oblique lines in the logo resemble the rain drops, used as a consistent element in the identity system. Coffee beans represent the exploration of not only the flavors around the world, but also the art of sensation, and therefore, the studio employed a black hole, a geometric shape, to interpret the idea of "Explore more".

Designer Liu Qianling, Liu Qianli, Cao Sheng | Studio out.o studio | Client Raining Coffee

埃塞俄比亚 Ethiopia
6 • 10g

explore
more
with
raining
6 • 10g
drip bag coffee

explore
more
with
raining

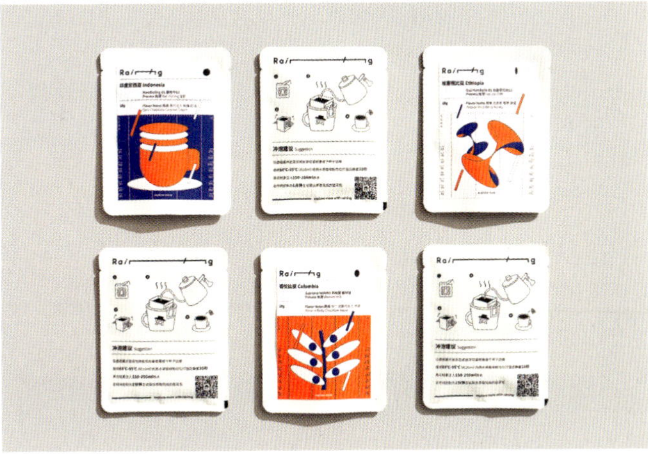

Brochure of University Arts Centre of the CUHK-Shenzhen

University Arts Centre of the Chinese University of Hong Kong, Shenzhen is committed to bridging the gap between students and arts. In the cover of the brochure, the studio interpreted the image of the center with simple geometric shapes, which originate from items related to people's impression of the center, like incubators or microphones, hoping to show the diverse culture of the center. Pages inside also feature abstract geometric shapes, which help the readers to know about different art activities of the center.

Designer Liu Qianling, Liu Qianli, Cao Sheng | Studio out.o studio

Client University Arts Centre of the CUHK-Shenzhen

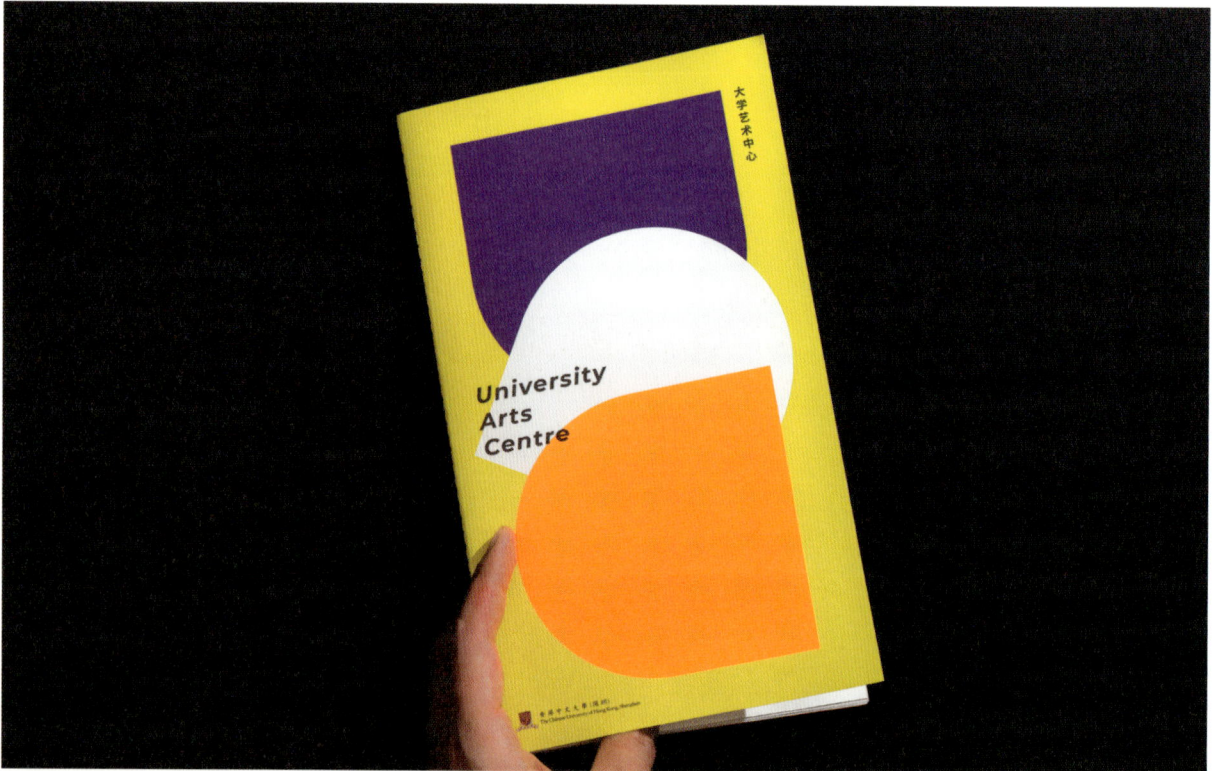

University Annual

Since 2015, in appre... and concern of peop... University of Hong K... concerts every year,... Longgang District G... principals from all o... University of Hong K... in Shenzhen and sto... music and at the sam... for the University.

Sparkle Music Festival

The Chinese University of Hong Kong, Shenzhen held the first Sparkle Music Festival in September of 2016 and the second one in January of 2018 aiming at promoting rock music on the University campus, and creating an opportunity for students with such interests to learn and communicate with the pro...

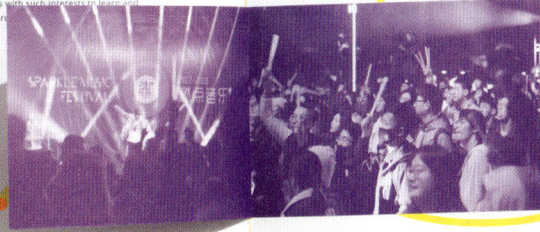

University Arts Centre   9   10   The Chinese University of Hong Kong, Shenzhen

Artist-in-Residence Project

In 2016, the University initiated the Artist-in-Residence Programme to create an artistic atmosphere on campus and to elevate student's aesthetic taste. We regularly invite top artists from various fields all over the world to reside on campus, create artworks and hold workshops with students.

The programme may last 5-10 days or 1-2 months. Artists will work with and guide students to create or appreciate artworks through workshops or lectures. Artists will also take into account resources available off campus to contribute towards our development. Until the end of 2018, 15 artists from different regions and various art fields have participated in the programme.

University Arts Centre   3   4   The Chinese University of Hong Kong, Shenzhen

out.o studio 2020 New Year Red Envelope

This is a New Year red envelope of 2020 decided for the members of out.o studio. The red envelope, with the theme of "Let's Stay Together", features a star-shape illustration, which means that everyone in the studio is a star, and together they will be brighter than ever in the coming year.

Designer Liu Qianling, Liu Qianli, Cao Sheng | Studio out.o studio

LESS IS MORE.
— LUDWIG MIES VAN DER ROHE

LESS

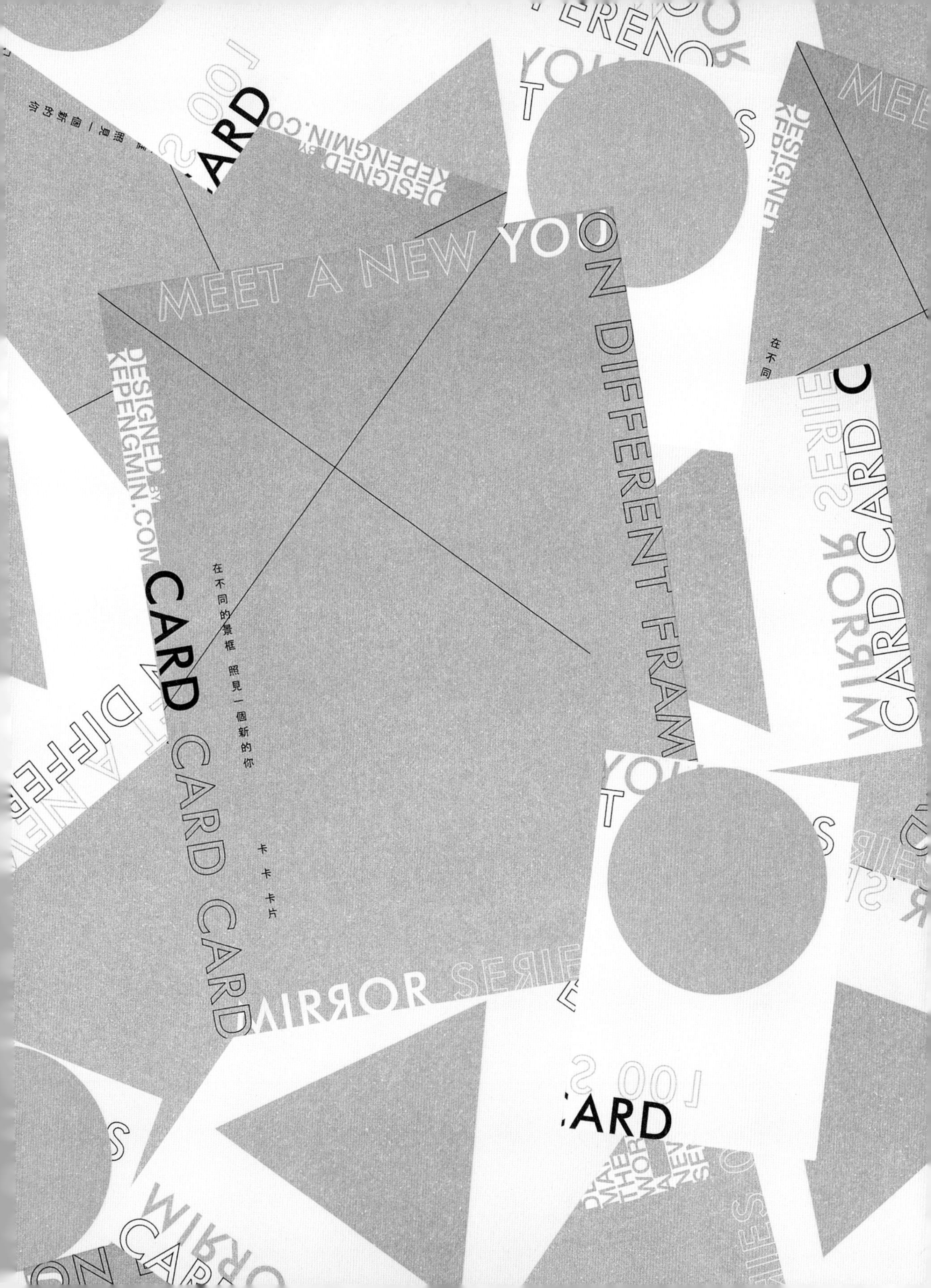

CARD

MEET A NEW YOU

DESIGNED BY
XEPENGMIN.COM

CARD
CARD CARD CARD

ON DIFFERENT FRAM

在不同的景框 照見一個新的你

卡 卡 卡 片

DESIGNED BY
XEPENGMIN.COM

在不同

CARD
MIRROR SERIE

MIRROR SERIE

LOOS 001

CARD

Mirror
Series
001

Mirror Series is a project resembling the journey of self-discovery in the age flooded with information. The project starts with Card Card Card, a design with its name, size and other elements all focusing on the number "3". Three cards each contain three geometric shapes — square, triangle and circle, which implies the frame of a mirror. The designer chose spot color printing, and had the design printed in silver on an uncoated paper from Antalis to present the mirror.

Designer Ke Pengmin | Studio Kepengmin Studio

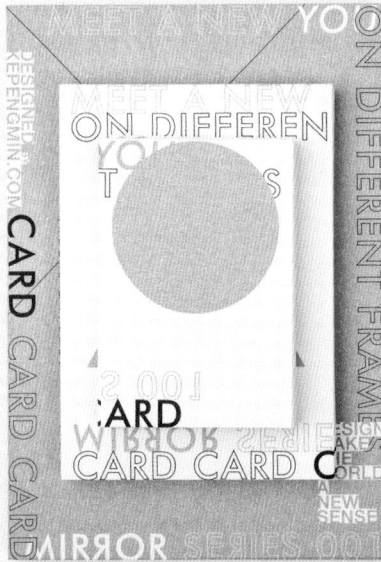

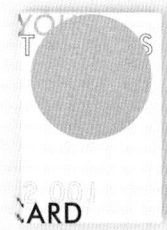

Orange and Lemon Tea

This is a packaging design for ice tea. The packaging design of the tea aims at telling its audience directly and visually about its natural ingredients, its unique producing process and its high quality. The illustrations are colorful and lively, while giving people a feeling of calm and delicacy, which establishes a rather refreshing image of ice tea.

Designer & illustrator Morten Kantsø

Kutsurogi no onboraato

The designer wanted to give a deep impression to the audience within a limited space of the bottle label, and ended up using three-dimensional effect to build up a direct visual result. The design is very helpful in boosting the sales volume, and the sale would end when all the stock is sold out.

Designer Naoko Fukuoka | Studio woolen | Client FUKUMITSUYA

Credit/ Debit Card Series

The designer thinks it would be fun and joyful to have something different on the credit/ debit cards. Besides the slightly unusual visual outcome, working with basic geometric shapes and a bright color palette enables the card to stand out with special visual effects. The simple combinations of geometric elements were built by transforming the card format into a grid, filling it with a mix of various geometric shapes. For the colors, the aim was to produce a palette where all colors could be consistent as the brief was to create a series.

Designer Gregory Page | Studio Pigment

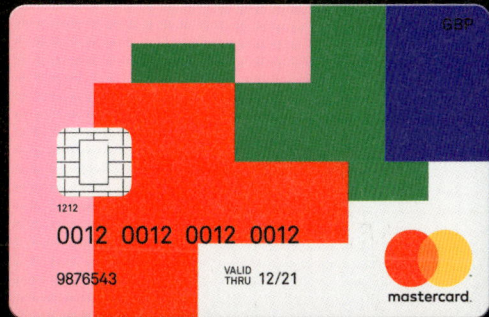

IS THERE ANY PROJECT YOU INVOLVED IN THAT NATURALLY MAKES YOU FEEL LIKE GOING WITH GEOMETRIC ELEMENTS?

Götz Gramlich

Basic geometric shapes are a good choice in design. They help the viewer to quickly decipher the designer's idea and they are very eye-catching.

Lung-Hao Chiang

Actually, I tend to try geometric shapes in each of my design projects to break down visual elements, so I can focus on organizing and designing. I believe that using symbols in design is very helpful to allow the object to stand out to be remembered. The theme of the design is rather highlighted when geometric elements and abstract symbols are used in the layout, which enables the designer to better communicate the information.

Alpoher Studio

My poster design process always involves some sort of geometrical elements. I think it feels natural to me to start my design process with playing and experimenting how shapes interact with each other and how colors can affect those shapes. At the beginning, this process appears to be really simple but at the same time super complex. I really like this design process where geometry is the starting point of laying down information. I have been taught to think with shapes and to simplify the design as much as possible, so I try to start every project based on that principle. When it comes to design, I found that poster and music-related design are where I go for geometry the most. Geometry is to me the best way to express and simplify a song or a mood into shapes and is where I can boldly play with shapes and turn the project into a very fun design process.

Josh Harris

Naturally when I work on branding projects and logo designs, my mind goes straight to geometric elements. Having a basic understanding of different shapes and the psychology behind them allows you to create work which best represents the brand and how the brand wishes to be seen. They have the ability to symbolize moods, ideas and philosophies and through this we can change the way a brand is perceived, simply through the shape of their logo or shapes used throughout their branding. Different shapes can all convey and communicate different messages so it is important we understand and apply them correctly.

Scandinavian Design Group

I like to explore geometric shapes when working on type designs, posters or brand identities. Creating visual systems around geometric shapes is relevant both for form and function.

Gregory Page

The credit/debit card project featured in this book and more recently a display typeface called Eclect that was released in spring 2021, which was based on a few main geometric shapes, mixing angles and curves that were repeated, assembled or even slightly distorted to create all the necessary glyphs (alphabet, numbers, signs...).
A lot of my type researches is based or starts with basic geometric forms and evolves to something more complex or even more organic.

Nick Barclay

A lot of my printing designs use geometric elements, as they always add an extra layer of meaning and fun and bring in pops of color.

Yuka Shiramoto

I have dealt with a lot of package design works, and I often use geometric patterns for package design. Take food packaging as an example. I usually use geometric patterns as tool to express the color and taste of the product, and the combination of colors and shapes are designed based on what the product aims at giving to its audience. I also sometimes employ certain delicately designed geometric patterns to help the product to stand out at the store shelves.

out.o studio

When we were considering how to start the project Raining Coffee, we thought of making "rain" the major visual element in the design, which naturally led us to use vertical lines to represent rain, because "raining" in the brand name is something very real. But in reality, influenced by wind, raindrops seldom fall vertically, so we tilted the lines. In the logo, the letter "n" was abstracted into an eave from which the raindrops fall. And the simple shape of the eave in the logo can be stretched or shortened to adapt different formats, which also symbolizes that the owner of the brand traveled around the world for high-quality coffee bean.

Ayaka Shimizu

Projects make me feel like to go with geometric elements are those need to convey something abstract and sensuous, but not something that gives a definite impression.

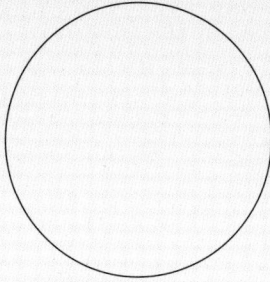

Subin Choi

Take my design, the poster for the Public Worry Project as an example. It is a program where teenagers hear the concerns of people through art like drawings. So at first, I tried to render the elements of drawing and worries with specific illustrations. But they were too figural and specific, so I decided to express this in different ways. I believed that it would be better to use geometric elements to express the bright and energetic energy of teenagers. Therefore, I used curves and diverse colors of circles as the main graphic elements in the poster.

STUDIO NA.EO

We have two steps in dealing with projects. First, we dig down into the culture behind the project, which is somewhat like the process of editorial design; second, we try to find a symbol system that matches the brand philosophy, aiming to present the design in symbols, and in this way, meaning will be given to the design. In fact, we tend to try geometric shapes in every design project, but how to present the project in visual language mainly depends on the needs of the brand.

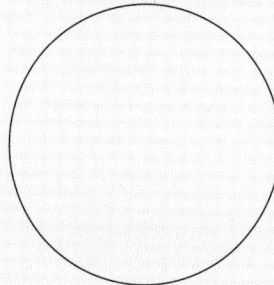

Makebardo

We recently finished a honey branding project whose identity was based on the honeycombs (hexagonal pattern). Although the hexagonal morphology may seem simplistic and overused in this category, we used it differently than expected. We behaved like bees when we developed all the identity. In nature, the hexagonal cells serve as storage vessels for honey and homes to raise young bees; this results in open and capped honey cells. We used this consequence of nature's behavior as a resource, so we used the full and empty cell to build the brand identity. We achieved a coherent, exciting and non-cliche visual story. To resume, we knew that there were geometries used in excess for their symbolism in specific categories, so the challenge was not to "not use them" but to give them a different and unique approach.

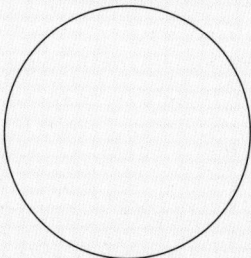

THE PICTORIAL
WORK WAS BORN OF
MOVEMENT, IS ITSELF
RECORDED MOVEMENT,
AND IS ASSIMILATED
THROUGH MOVEMENT
(EYE MUSCLES).
— PAUL KLEE

ARC XIX

The Avenue
Manchester, England

Sheppard Robson
2011

ARC

The ARC research project was a decomposition study to identify geometric patterns in architecture all around the world, conceptualizing the apparent Euclidean into two-dimensional patterns. A total of 25+ geometric patterns were created and presented in black and white posters. Each one includes a reference to the architecture's name, its location, the year it was built, and the architect.

Designer Xtian Miller

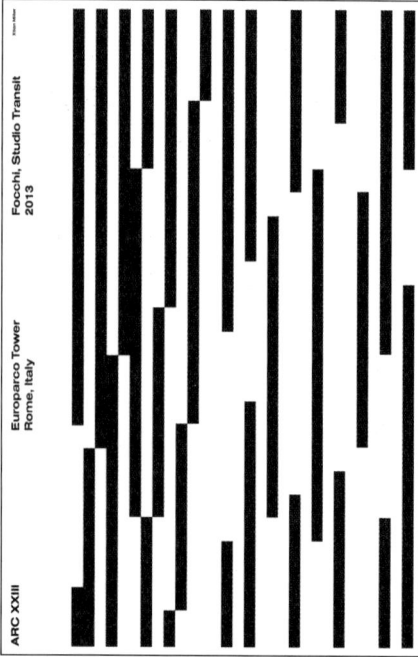

ARC XXIII

Europarco Tower
Rome, Italy

Focchi, Studio Transit
2013

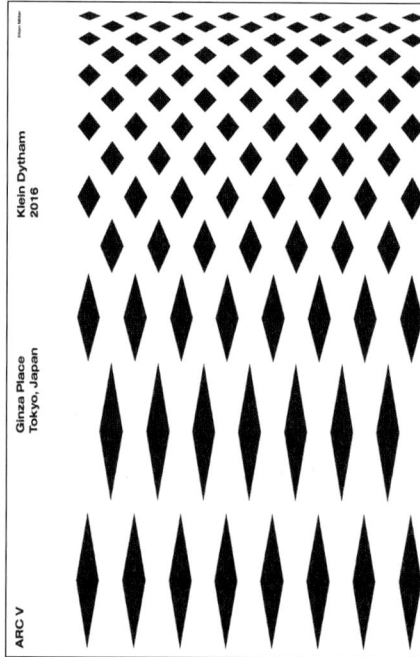

ARC V

Ginza Place
Tokyo, Japan

Klein Dytham
2016

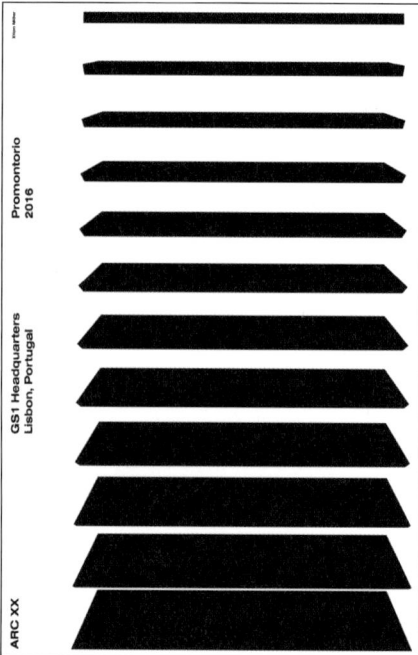

ARC XX

GS1 Headquarters
Lisbon, Portugal

Promontorio
2016

ARC XIV

Central Bank of Ireland
London, England

Henry J Lyons
2017

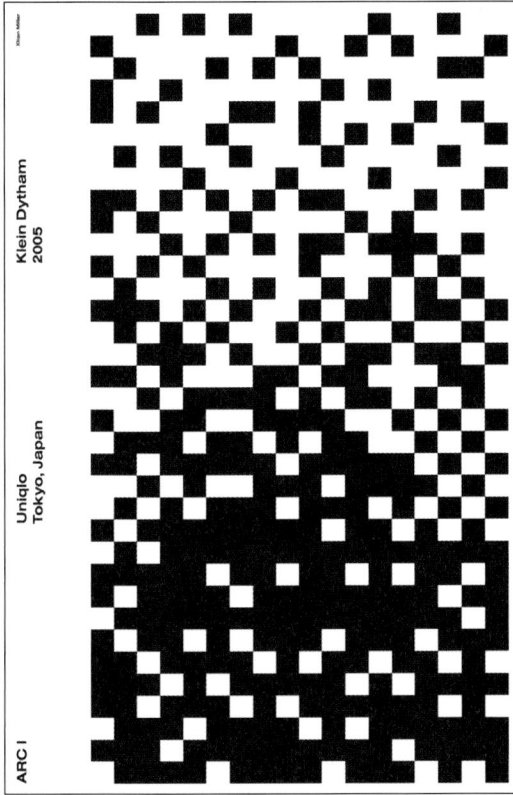

ARC I

Klein Dytham
2005

Uniqlo
Tokyo, Japan

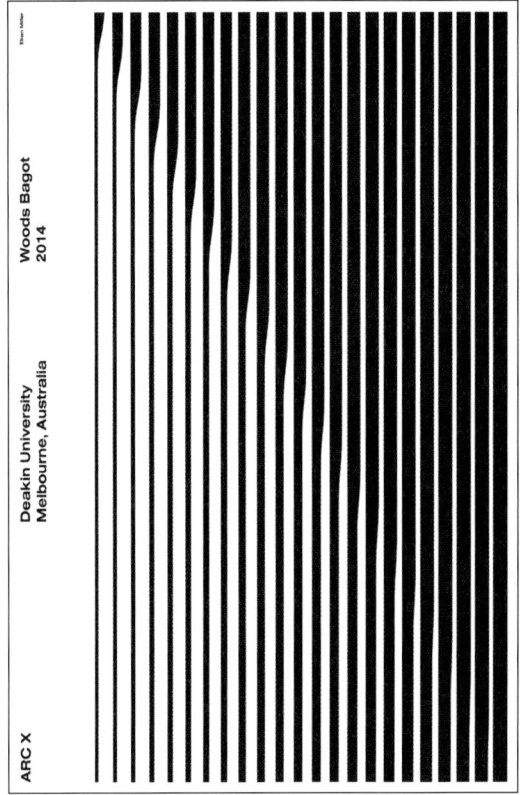

ARC X

Woods Bagot
2014

Deakin University
Melbourne, Australia

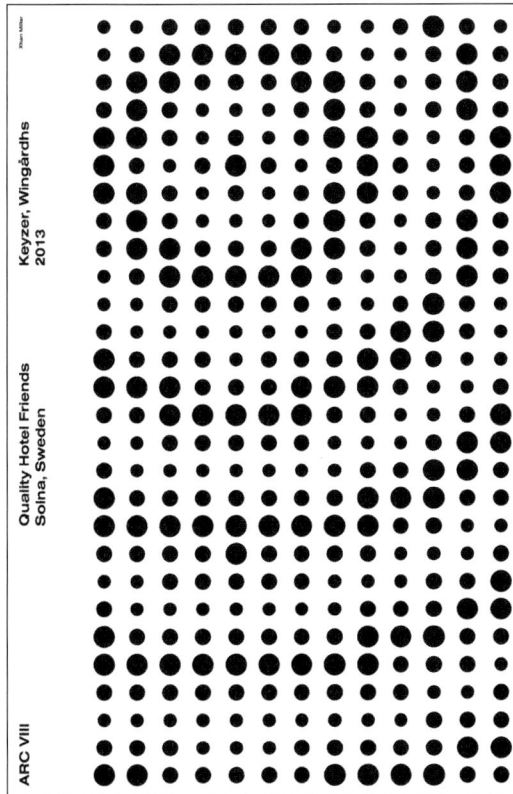

ARC VIII

Keyzer, Wingårdhs
2013

Quality Hotel Friends
Solna, Sweden

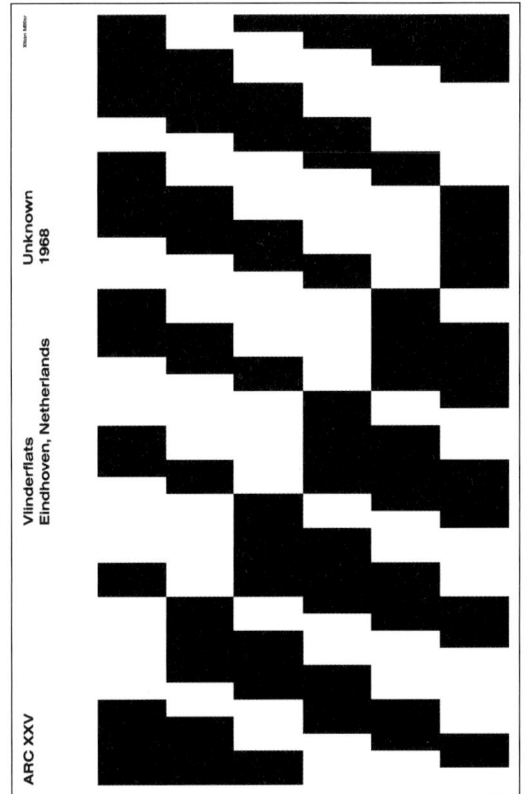

ARC XXV

Unknown
1968

Vlinderflats
Eindhoven, Netherlands

Form Research

Inspired by the Op Art, the designer has been constantly carrying out researches about the using of geometric shapes, like circle, square and triangle since November, 2019.

Designer Fatih Hardal | Studio Hardal Studio

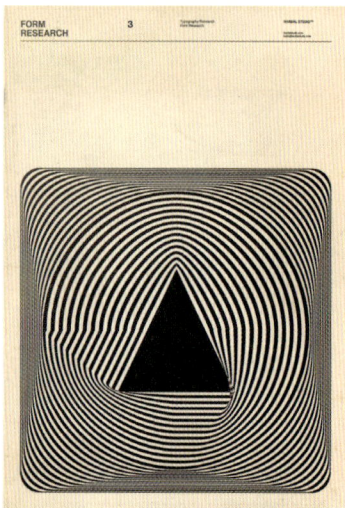

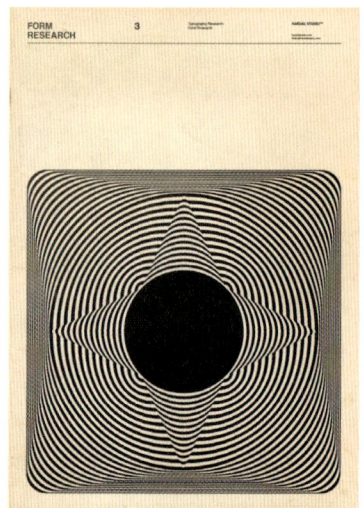

Geometry Now !

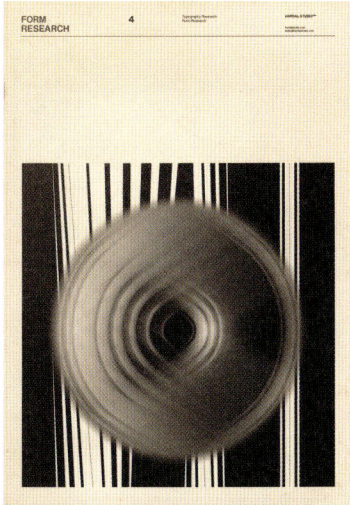

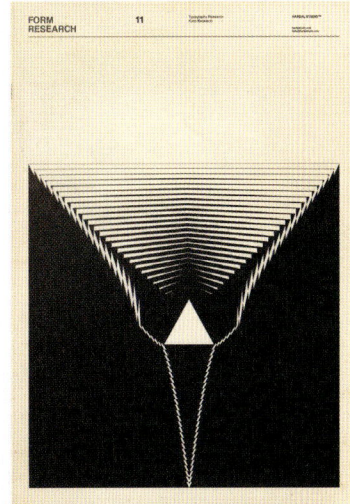

THE PURPOSE OF ART IS TO RE-PRESENT NATURE, NOT REPRESENT IT.
— JOSEF ALBERS

NATURE

Rain shower
rain pattern specimen
Design Summer 7 workshop

Drizzling rain
rain pattern specimen
Design Summer 7 workshop

Rainy season
rain pattern specimen
Design Summer 7 workshop

Puddle
rain pattern specimen
Design Summer 7 workshop

Clouds and rain
rain pattern specimen
Design Summer 7 workshop

Rain Pattern Specimen

Rain Pattern Specimen is a series of postcards with 16 different rain patterns. The designer used various illustration techniques to express the seasonal rains in Japan.

Designer Hiroko Sakai | Studio coton design

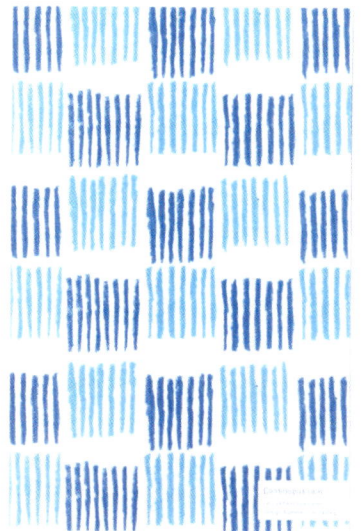

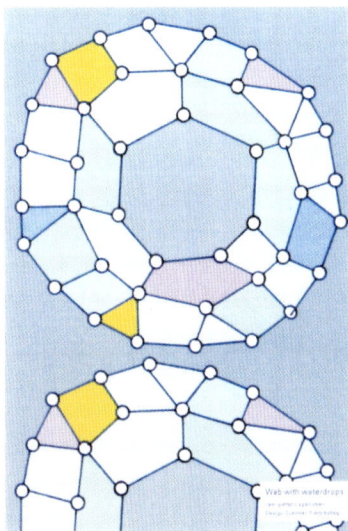

AdataAiR

ADATA Artist-in-Residence (AdataAiR) program is a series of artistic interventions in the urban environment of Plovdiv, Bulgaria. The visual identity aims to show the importance of a cardinal unit in the project, the river island Adata — a metaphor for an isolated urban landscape that can be enlivened through culture, dialogue and interaction. It operates as a symbol of potential and change. Therefore, the image of the island does not remain static in the visual identity — it is constantly changing its structure, interacting with images and graphics, making the connection between the environment and man, and rediscovering its diversity.

Studio PUNKT | Client Plovdiv 2019 European Capital of Culture

Geometry Now !

The Forest Gems

The inspiration came from watching the coffee in the cup glittered brilliantly in the sunlight like amber gems in the cup. The designer hopes to combine the elegant and precious product image of specialty coffee with precious gem. The coffee cherries glitter in the sunlight and morning dew like gems in the forest. The packaging design hopes to visualize the aroma of coffee and the elegance of precious gems, combining the texture of the cut face of the gem with a metallic color, creating coffee is the glittered gem in the forest.

Designer Lung-Hao Chiang

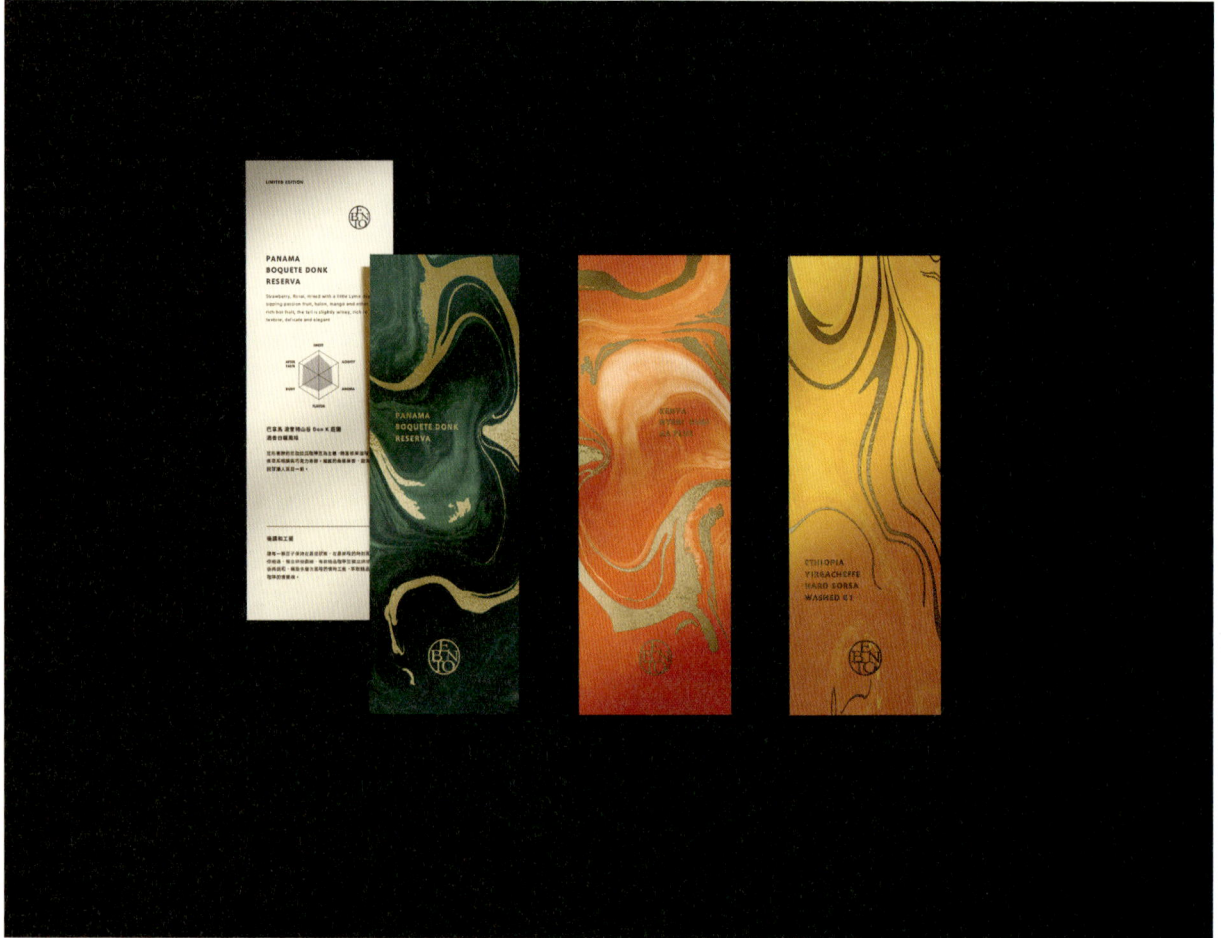

THE MIND IS LIKE AN UMBRELLA — IT FUNCTIONS BEST WHEN OPEN.
— WALTER GROPIUS

OPEN

Check Your Breasts Regularly

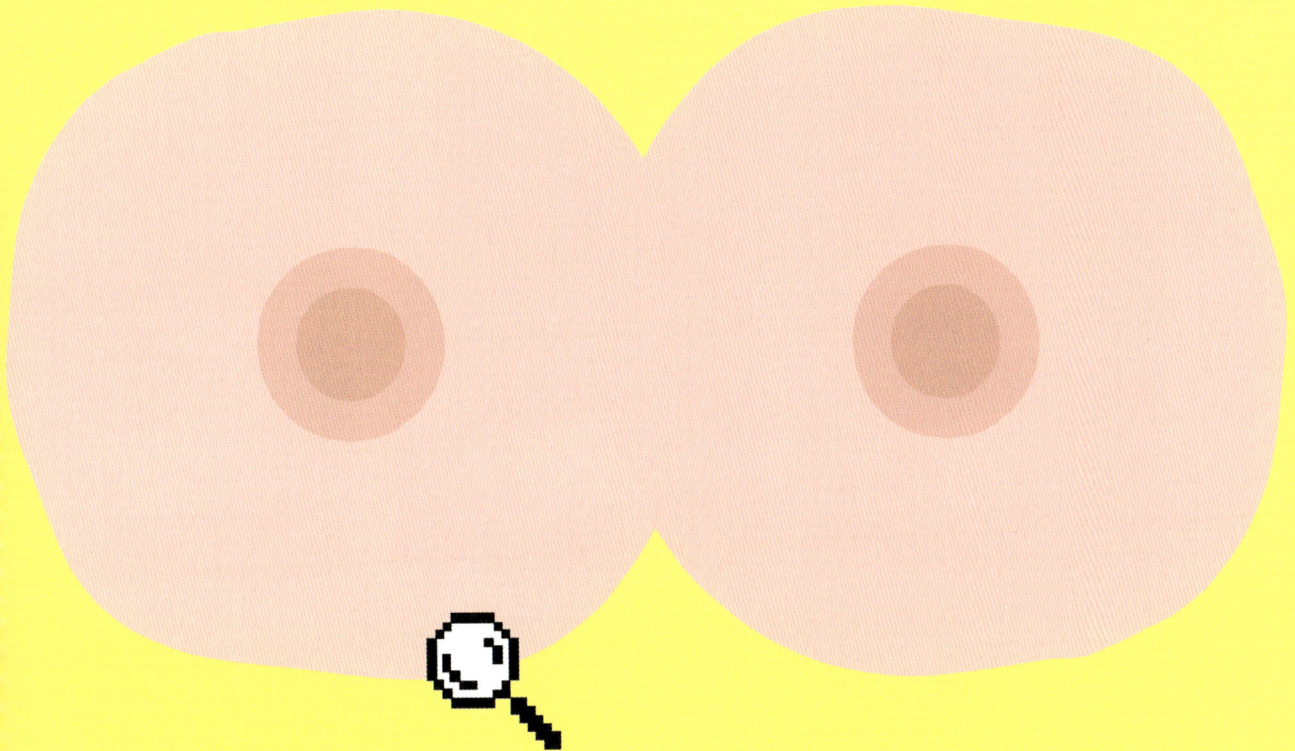

Reviving the Traditional Culture — Suichang Zongzi

The studio launches a project named Reviving the Traditional Culture, which aims at breaking the stereotype about package designs of traditional items by adopting a bold visual language. The project starts with the package design of Suichang Zongzi. The designer, according to different flavors of the Zongzi, uses various abstract geometric shape combinations, with a bold color scheme and typeface. Made of an elegant and environmentally friendly paper, and presented by spot color printing, the delicately designed package box of Suichang Zongzi revives the traditional culture in a brand new visual context.

Designer Totoro | Studio Faceupdesign Studio

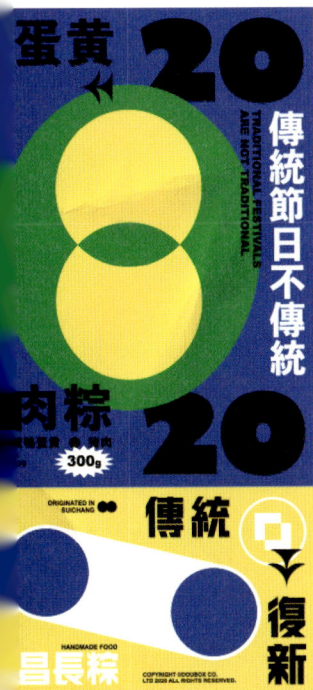

A Lesson in Texture & Colour

This poster collection is an in-house experimentation project that plays not only with colors but also with shapes and textures. The idea of this series of posters is to represent the contrast and balances between geometrical and irregular shapes, which are all combined with bright colors and textures. In this exercise, the studio inversed the usual design process; the shapes respond to the colors and the textures.

^{Designer} Bren Imboden & Luis Viale | ^{Studio} makebardo

**A LESSON
IN TEXTURE
& COLOUR**

ENROL NOW
FOR 2016

soooon.co.nz

**A LESSON
IN TEXTURE
& COLOUR**

ENROL NOW
FOR 2016

soooon.co.nz

Check Your Breasts Regularly

October is the Breast Cancer Awareness Month, and makebardo collaborated with the cause through a digital awareness campaign. The decision to work with an organic and straightforward illustration was to give a personal approach to the message. The design is inclusive and uses bright colors to call attention because "early detection saves lives".

^{Designer} Bren Imboden & Luis Viale | ^{Studio} makebardo

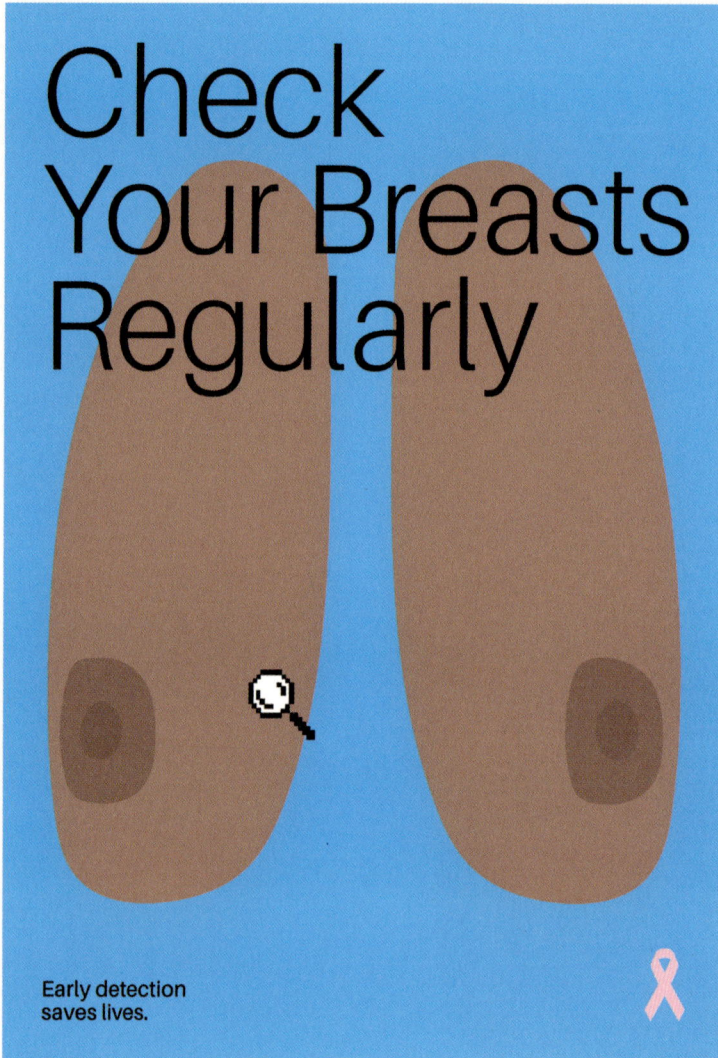

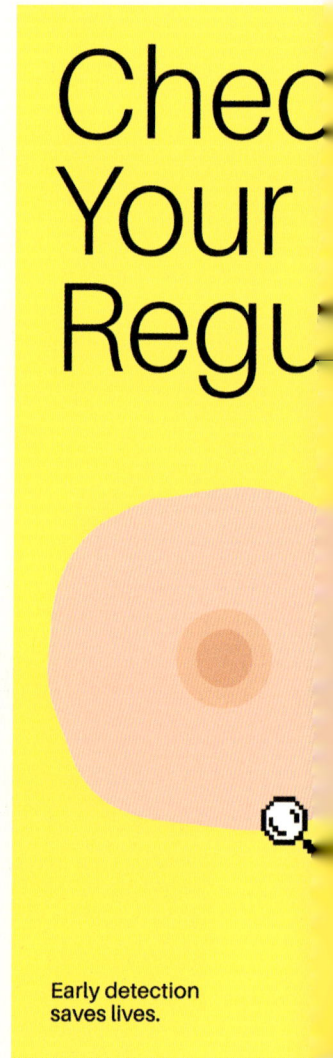

Check Your Breasts Regularly

Early detection saves lives.

Check Your Regu

Early detection saves lives.

Check Your Breasts Regularly

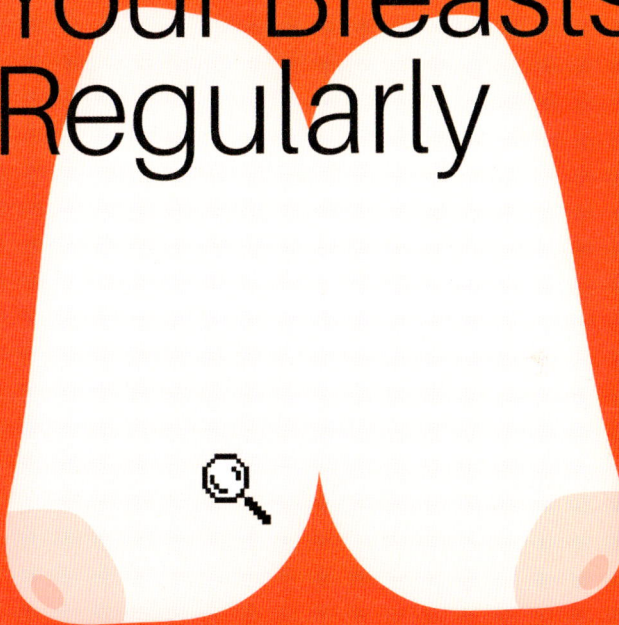

Early detection saves lives.

ART IS
POLYMORPHIC.
A PICTURE
APPEARS TO
EACH ONLOOKER
UNDER A
DIFFERENT GUISE.
— GEORGES BRAQUE

POLYMORPHIC

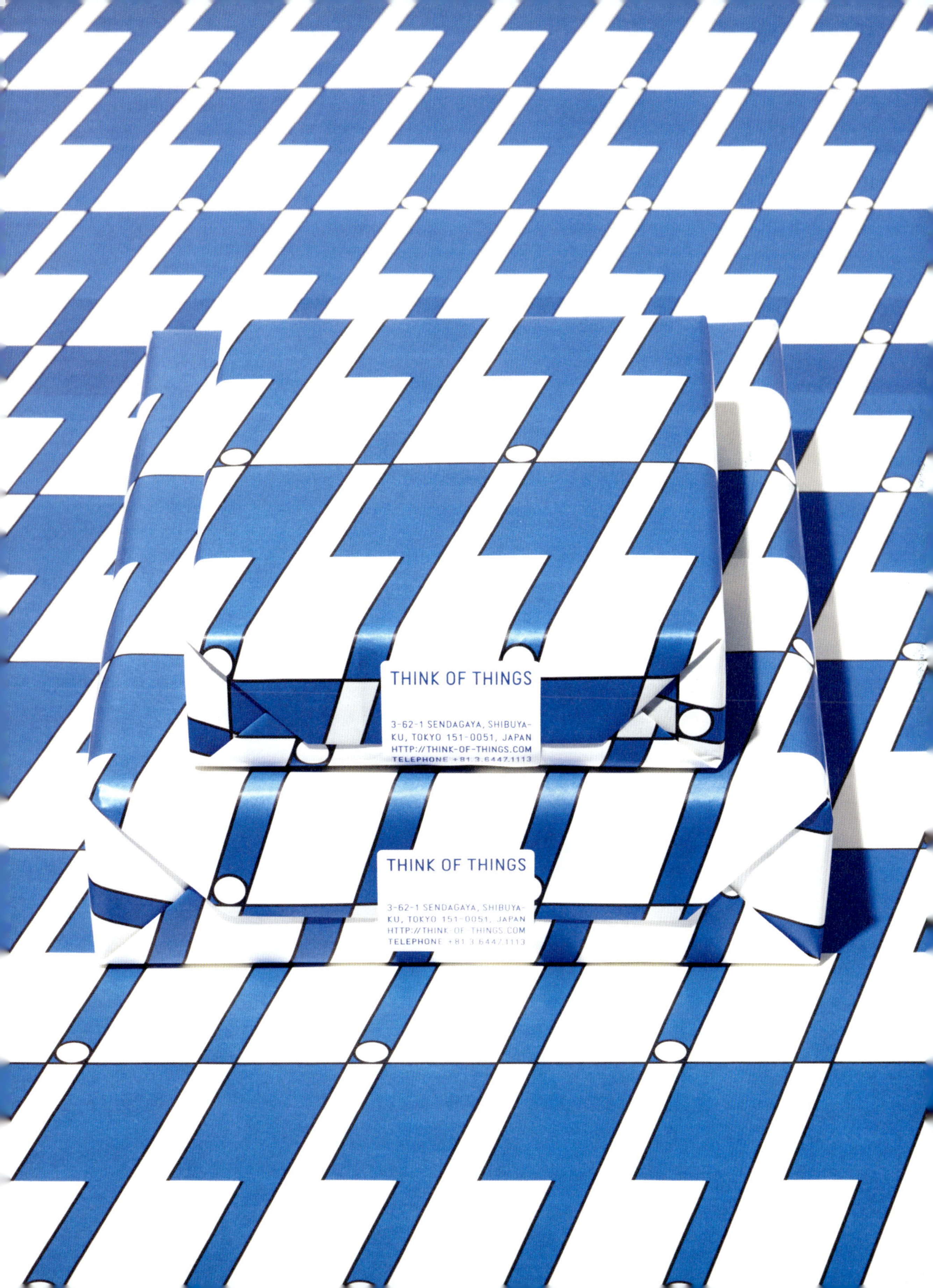

THINK OF THINGS

3-62-1 SENDAGAYA, SHIBUYA-
KU, TOKYO 151-0051, JAPAN
HTTP://THINK-OF-THINGS.COM
TELEPHONE +81.3.6447.1113

THINK OF THINGS

3-62-1 SENDAGAYA, SHIBUYA-
KU, TOKYO 151-0051, JAPAN
HTTP://THINK-OF-THINGS.COM
TELEPHONE +81.3.6447.1113

THINK
OF
THINGS

THINK OF THINGS is a shop and café operated by KOKUYO, a Japanese stationery and office furniture manufacturer. The THINK OF THINGS logo and the identity design employ letters and numbers, aiming at representing KOKUYO's trustworthy image of pursuing high quality. The logo is a simplification of the acronym, "TOT", which takes various forms in various combinations of different colors and shapes. The variations, on the other hand, imply different ways of thinking, and also the name of the brand, THINK OF THINGS.

Designer Aki Kanai, Taku Sasaki | Studio YOHAK DESIGN STUDIO | Client KOKUYO

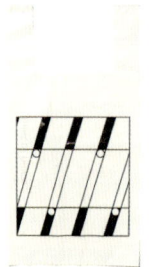

ICED COFFEE
WITH ORIGINAL BLEND

GUATEMALA AND
TANZANIA MIX

1,000ML

COLD BREW
WITH ETHIOPIA

BREW RATIO 1:10
BREW TIME 10H

200 ML

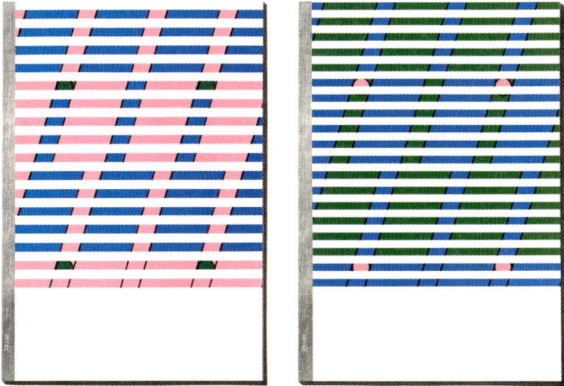

THINK OF THINGS

THINK OF THINGS

THINK OF THINGS

abC Art Book Fair 2020

abC (art book in China) is an independent book fair in China. Based on a dot matrix, the visual identity represents the possibility of a typeface, trying to present abC as a flexible independent art group that focuses on promoting art books. From dot to line and to plane, the elements in the design are combined randomly, forming different visual expressions that gradually go beyond the two dimensional plane, and eventually becoming the finest details of the visual identity.

Designer Liu Zhizhi, Mazzybox, Chen Chaohao | Studio STUDIO NA.EO |

Client abC Art Book Fair

EXHIBITOR
EXHIBITOR
EXHIBITOR
The 5th Art Book Fair 第五届
a b Beijing C 艺术书展
北京
07/24-07/26
第五 The 5th Art 届
艺术书展 a b Book
北京 07.24 C Fair
-07.26 Beijing

07/24-07/26

The 5th
a *b*
C
第五届
艺术书　　展
北京
Art
Book
Fair
Beijing

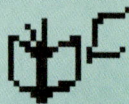

机构＆
媒体预展
Institutional
&
Media
Preview
2020
07.23
R.S.V.P

地址
Address
北京
时代美术馆
Beijing
Times
Art
Museum

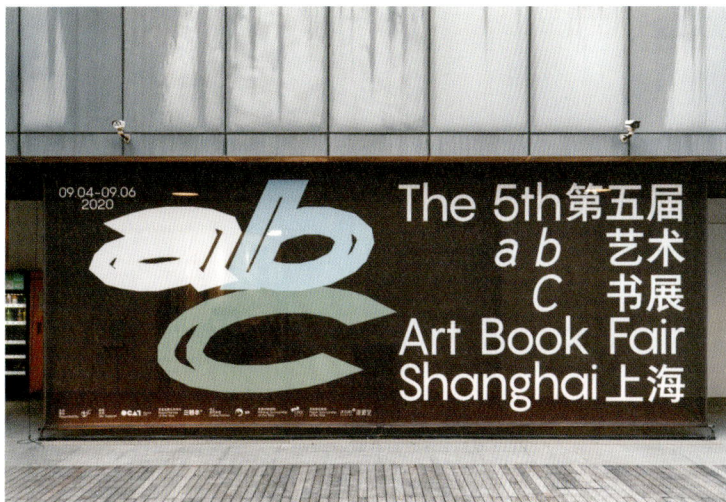

WHICH GEOMETRIC SHAPE IS THE MOST FREQUENTLY USED ONE IN YOUR DESIGN? OR WHICH GEOMETRIC SHAPE DO YOU OFTEN PREFER TO USE? DOES THIS DEPEND ON YOUR PERSONAL PREFERENCES OR SOMETHING ELSE?

Subin Choi

I generally use the circle most. It depends on the situation, but I often use circles based on my personal preferences. I love the feeling of curves from the circle. And the forms of the circle are interesting as well. A circle gives the impression of comfort and completeness. But it also gives a bright and energetic feeling depending on how it is placed. That's why I prefer the use of circles.

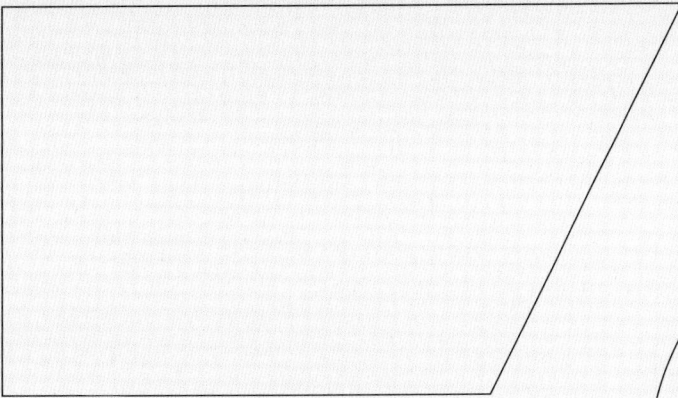

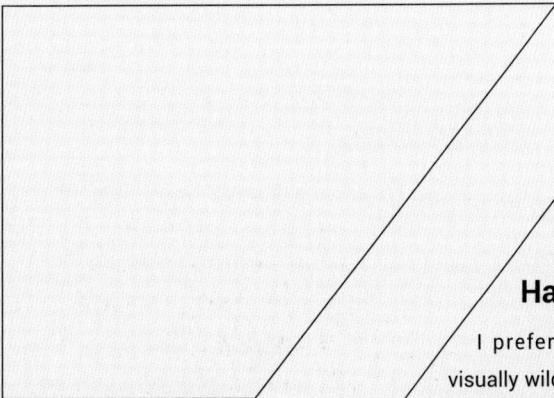

Johanne Lian Olsen

I love circles. These shapes are a great foundation for framing images and typography. They sit well on a page together with other elements and play well with the negative space around. I often incorporate this shape in my designs, whether I'm designing the shape or craft for a publication (rounded corners, die-cut holes), or informal framing of portraits in an editorial piece. The circle can highlight text content, be it large or small. Its simplicity makes it so versatile.

Götz Gramlich

My personal favorite of the simple geometric shape is undoubtedly the triangle. I love this pure form of asymmetry in the middle of a perfect balance. The three is a symbol for family and the simplest possible compromise. Two poles and a point in between open up a space.

Lung-Hao Chiang

I prefer shapes that are visually wild and striking, such as stars that boast a radial and polygonal structure which is quite attractive in visual language, and shapes with sharp angles, which, as I think, when used massively, allows an eye-catching yet elegant image.

Ke Pengmin

The most frequently used geometric shapes in my design are the three main basic ones, namely squares, triangles and circles. Any complex structure can be broke down into combinations of the three basic shapes.

Nick Barclay

I use circles a lot as I find them relaxing to work with and relaxing to look at and you don't have to deal with weird dead areas created by corners.

Zubin Jhaveri

I use triangles and shapes derived from it extensively in my designs. A triangle is quite versatile. You can create so many variations by just tweaking it a bit, changing the angles, making it thick or thin, longer or blunt. A more aggressive look can be achieved by merely making an angle more acute, while a more balanced design can be achieved by using equilateral triangles. It is my personal favorite and I have experimented it to get drastically different results. It is always exciting to see what more variations can be created next.

Alpoher Studio

I am not really sure. Talking about elemental shapes, I would say squares maybe. In terms of using them for design work, it really depends on the composition or the mood I want to pursue. Squares tend to be pretty cool to work with, you can create a lot of opportunities with them and they can develop a lot of variants with four vertices. I do not find myself tend to go with certain shape when it comes to preferences, but I guess I feel more comfortable with squares or circles. I find circles super interesting and attractive, as their infiniteness, their perfect round edge and their deepness and meaning are rather fascinating. I really enjoy circles too in my designs, but every shape I use I try to give it a meaning or a reason to be, so it really depends on what project I am doing.

Gregory Page

It is not an easy question, I would say the rectangle and the circle, maybe also a merge of these two (rectangle with rounded corners), which gives the rectangle a less strong feeling, a slight organic. Of course it depends on the legibility when and how to use a specific shape in regard of the concept and/or the context. These forms all carry a symbolic meaning, expressing different things. If I had to say which form I use rarely, it would be the pentagon, octagon… Maybe their complexity makes it more difficult to fit within a project, but this just a personal thought.

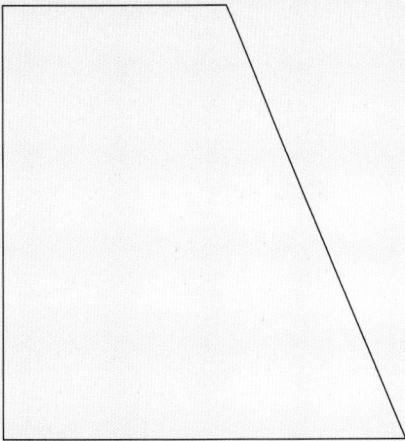

Yuka Shiramoto

I often use a combination of simple geometric shapes such as squares, triangles and circles. Combining simple figures and making various adjustments to elements such as size and color will make it possible for the design to express what it aims at communicating. In addition, simple geometric shapes are often used because it is easy to develop from one geometric design to various objects.

Ayaka Shimizu

I often use the ellipse, because it's softer than a polygon and more individual than a perfect circle.

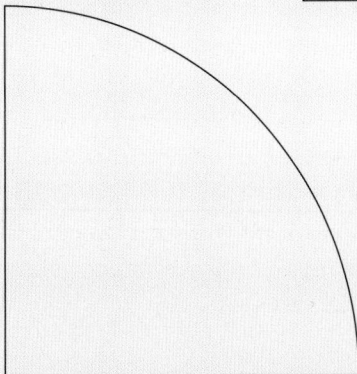

Makebardo

Of the primary geometric shapes, the one that recurs in our design is the circle. We do not prefer it over the others, but it is indeed the one we use the most. A possible explanation could be that our curiosity for the universe and the planets (undoubtedly represent through this geometry) flows into our design unconsciously and emotionally. We also feel inspired by the circle because of its absence of beginning or end, and its magnetic serenity.

THE FACTS SHOW THAT
IF EVEN THE HUMBLEST
PRODUCT IS DESIGNED,
MANUFACTURED, AND
DISTRIBUTED WITH A
SENSE OF HUMAN VALUES
AND WITH A TASTE FOR
QUALITY, THE WORLD
WILL RECOGNIZE THE
PRESENCE OF A CREATIVE
FORCE.
— HERBERT BAYER

QUALITY

Home cooked
meals in
15 min.

Gobble

Gobble

Gobble

Gobble

Gobble offers 15-minute gourmet dinners that customers can cook with a single pan. The project started with the wordmark, with the system to follow. It was important to create a fully custom wordmark for Gobble that built on their existing logo to preserve the brand equity. As the brand was so fun and lively, the studio believed that it needed to present information clearly and concisely for the customers, which allows them to quickly understand the steps needed to make their dinner. Therefore, the studio designed a restrained set of recipe cards that would fit inside the boxes, removing the patterns to allow the food to be the star of the show.

Studio Studio Mast | Photographer Scott Snyder | Client Gobble

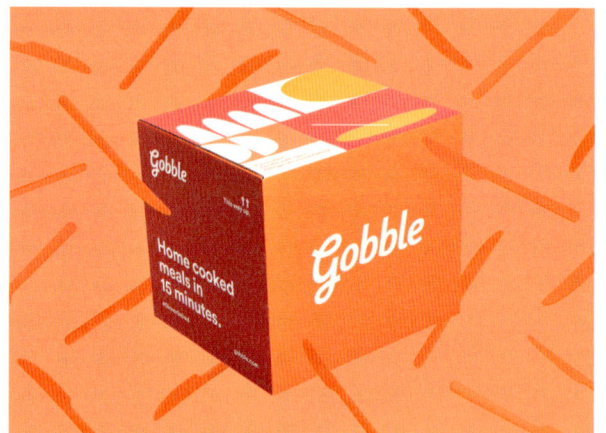

Kaleidoscope—
Paper Art

As kids we all loved looking into a Kaleidoscope and being entranced by the simple glass pieces unfolding into infinite mesmerizing designs. Trying to capture the pattern presented inside the Kaleidoscope, the designer tries to create something so captivating, something that would make the viewer feel fascinated and hypnotized as they try to decode the secrets the artwork holds.

Designer Zubin Jhaveri

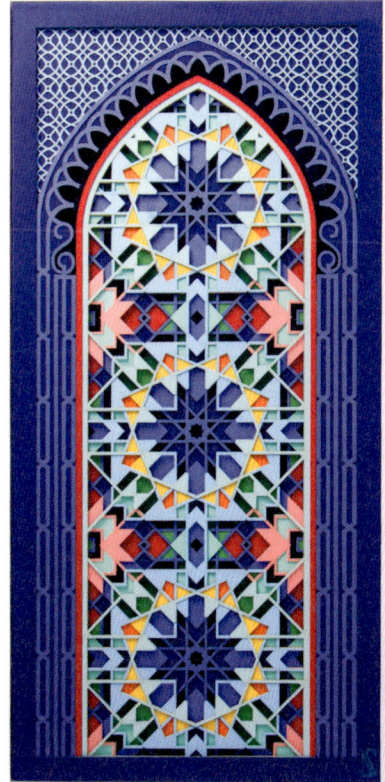

REDUCTION! ONE WANTS TO SAY MORE THAN NATURE AND ONE MAKES THE IMPOSSIBLE MISTAKE OF WANTING TO SAY IT WITH MORE MEANS THAN SHE, INSTEAD OF FEWER. — PAUL KLEE

REDUCTION

Repeat Repeat

This is a visual identity design for the London based art show *Repeat Repeat*. The exhibition explored the idea of repetition through shapes, patterns and colors. Artists Frea Buckler and Chris Page showcased works that exhibited their approach to repetition through different processes and techniques. To support the show's concept, a visual language was created with strong repetitive typography and patterns. The use of patterns and colors across all visual communications represented both the artists' artwork style. This visual language was used across promotional posters, social media content and the exhibition space.

Designer Chris Page

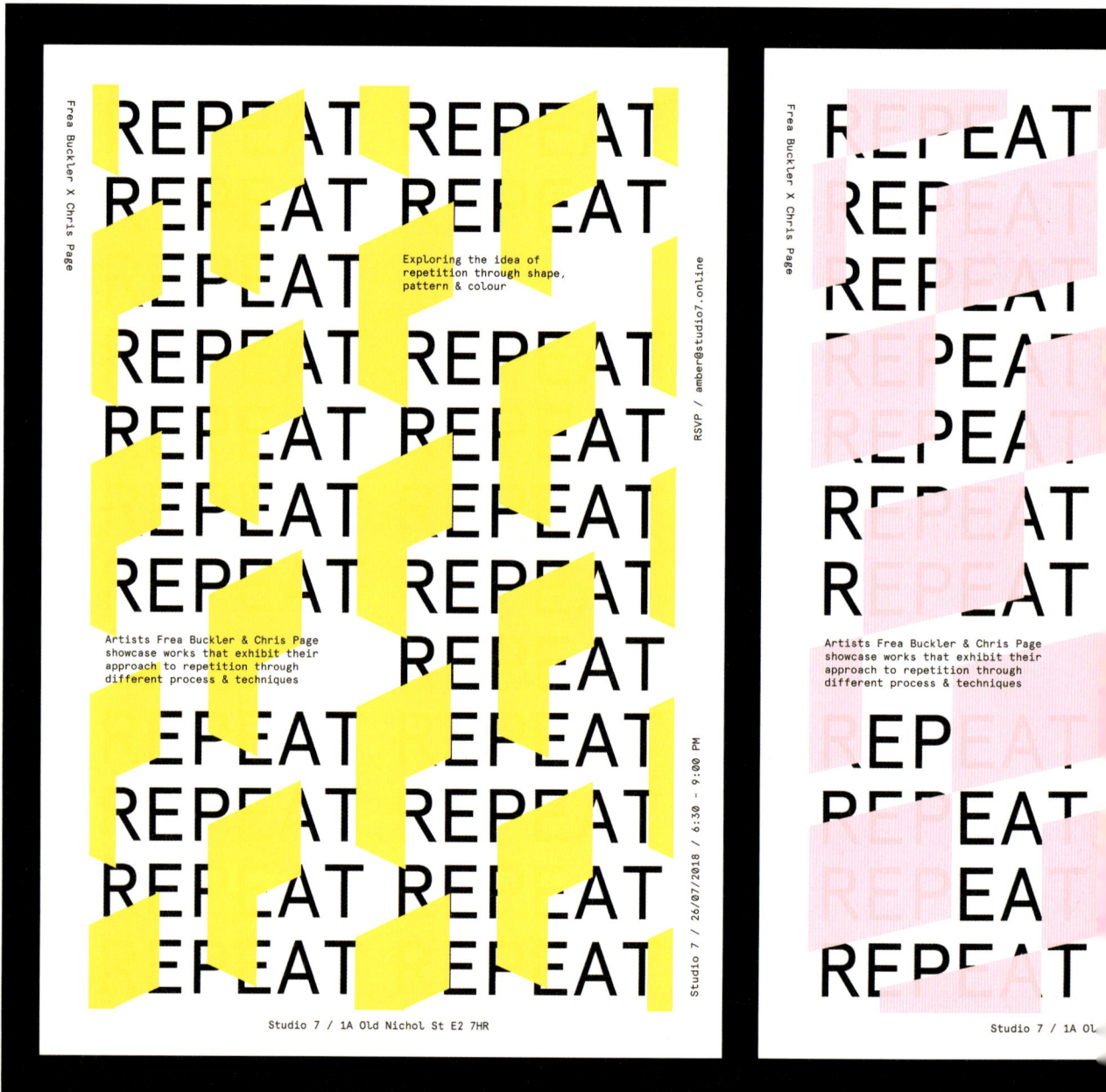

REPEAT REPEAT REPEAT REPEAT REPEAT REPEAT REPEAT REPEAT REPEAT REPEAT REPEAT REPEAT REPEAT REPEAT

Frea Buckler X Chris Page

Exploring the idea of repetition through shape, pattern & colour

Artists Frea Buckler & Chris Page showcase works that exhibit their approach to repetition through different process & techniques

RSVP / amber@studio7.online

Studio 7 / 26/07/2018 / 6:30 - 9:00 PM

Studio 7 / 1A Old Nichol St E2 7HR

Frea Buckler X Chris Page

Artists Frea Buckler & Chris Page showcase works that exhibit their approach to repetition through different process & techniques

Studio 7 / 1A OL

the idea of
through shape,
colour

RSVP / amber@studio7.online

Studio 7 / 26/07/2018 / 6:30 - 9:00 PM

7HR

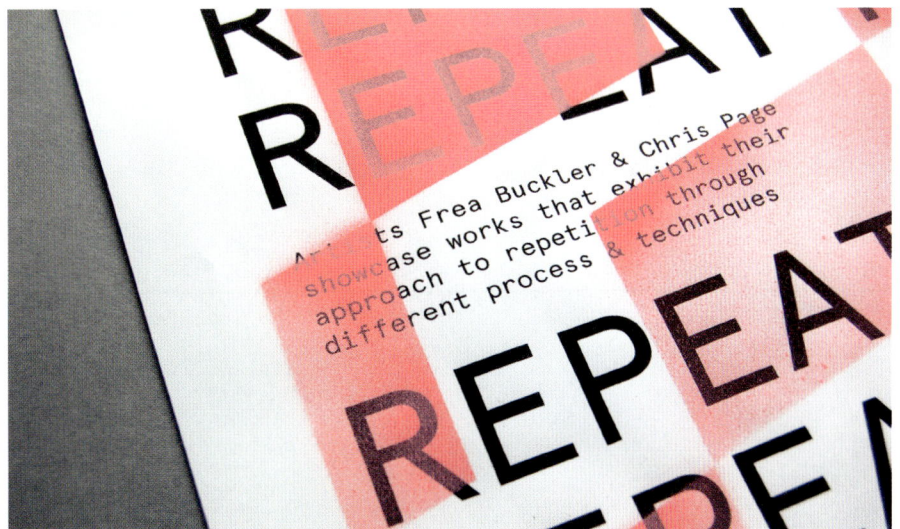

Artists Frea Buckler & Chris Page showcase works that exhibit their approach to repetition through different process & techniques

Round-the-Clock Pizza Box

After 30 years of delivering pizzas during regular hours, Toronto's Seven West Restaurant went 24/7. To tell pizza lovers that pizza time is any time, we designed 12 custom boxes — one for each hour, day or night. So, if you ordered pizza at 1 pm, you learned that the same deliciousness was available at 1 am. Boxes went out at the corresponding time.

Designer Man Wai Wong | Studio Leo Burnett Design | Client 7 West Restaurant

The box reads:

PIZZA TIME
IS ANY TIME

BECAUSE YOU'RE 5 HOURS INTO A NETFLIX
SERIES ABOUT FOOD, ATE EVERYTHING IN
YOUR PANTRY, AND STILL HUNGRY

BECAUSE A CO-WORKER, PROBABLY ONE OF
THOSE ANIMALS FROM FINANCE, STOLE YOUR
LUNCH OUT OF THE OFFICE FRIDGE.

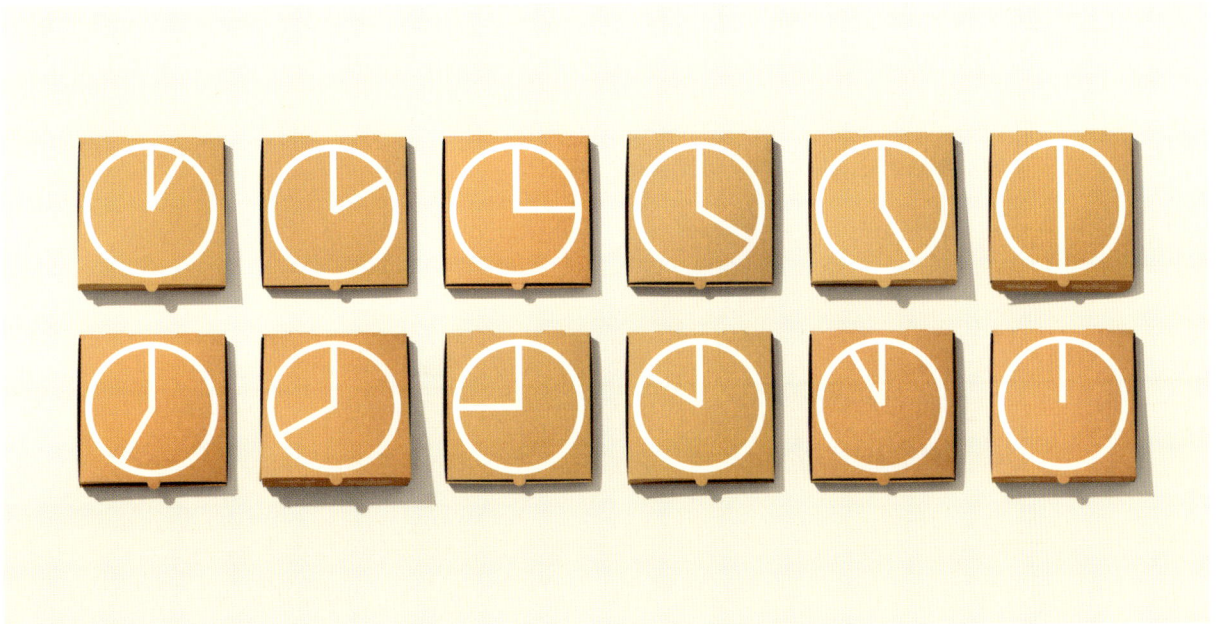

Armonía Wines

The studio worked on the branding, labels and promotional material for a new Spanish wine company, Armonía. Armonía were looking for a contemporary look to help the brand stand out within the market. The studio achieved this with the use of bright colors and bold patterns that were rarely seen within the wine industry.

Designer Eddie Cooper | Studio 2Fold Studio | Client Armonía Wines

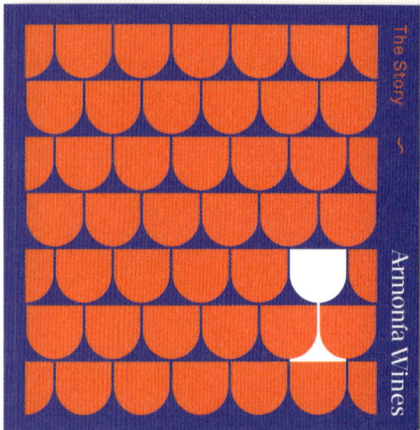

AS WE DO NOT SEE SQUARES IN NATURE, I THOUGHT THAT IT IS MAN-MADE. BUT I HAVE CORRECTED MYSELF. BECAUSE SQUARES EXIST IN SALT CRYSTALS, OUR DAILY SALT. — JOSEF ALBERS

SQUARE

ONSITE

ONSITE SUPPLY + DESIGN
LEVEL 1, 17 ROYLSTON STREET
PADDINGTON NSW 2021
TELEPHONE: 02 9360 3666

INFO@ONSITESD.COM.AU

WWW.ONSITESD.COM.AU

O

TILE & STO

INFO@ON

Onsite

This is a branding project for Onsite, a tile & stone merchant based in Sydney. The idea was to produce a clean high end feel and use geometric shapes to represent the different tiles they supply.

Designer Nick Barclay | Studio Nick Barclay Designs | Client Onsite

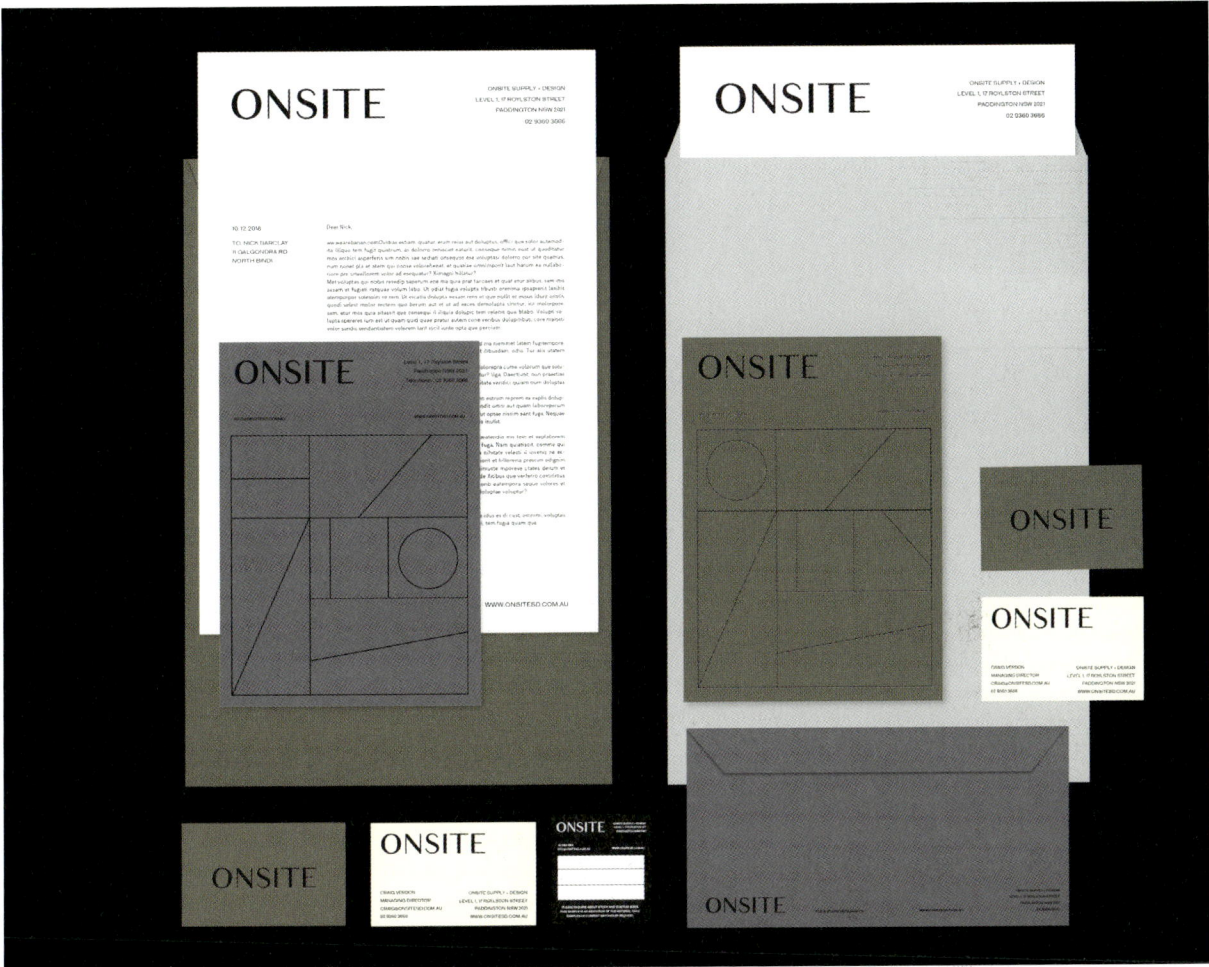

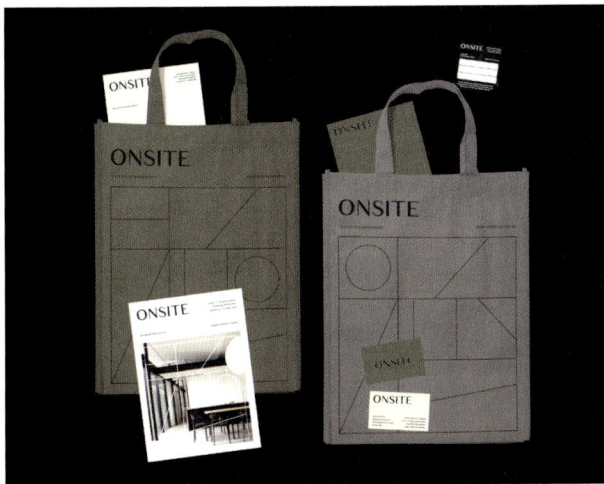

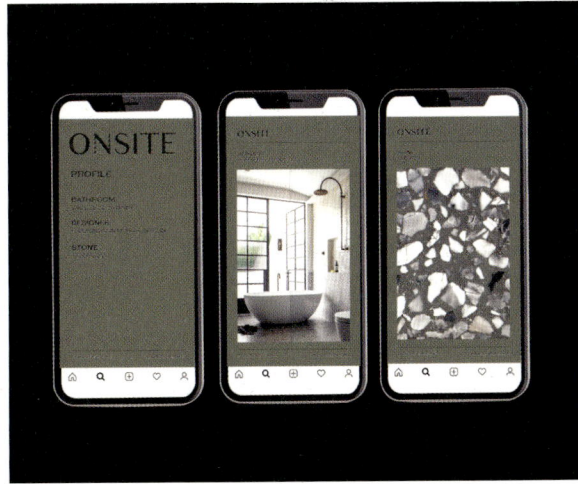

Time and Space

Time and Space is a personal project. The idea came from the second chapter, "The Time of a Witch" of *The Words of a Witch* (Wuyan), a novel by Zhu Tianwen. When talking about the end of love, the author mentioned Italo Calvino's digression — digression is a strategy for putting off the ending, a multiplying of time within the work, a perpetual evasion or flight. Turning time into space while feeling the way through the complexity was a metaphor the author left in the novel.

Designer Ke Pengmin | Studio Kepengmin Studio | Client Time and Space

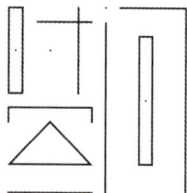

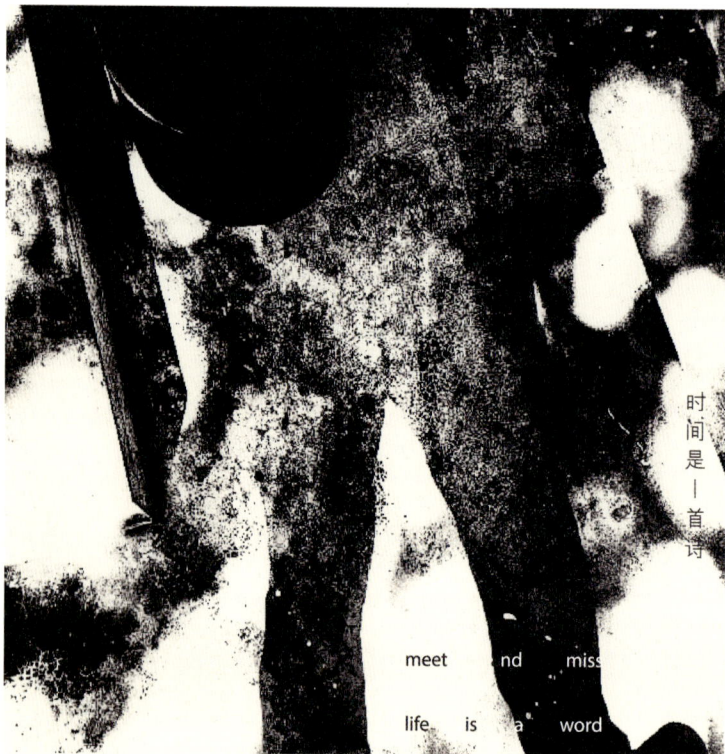

时间是一首诗

生命是一句话

遇见与错过

TIME AND SPACE

meet and miss

life is a word

time is like a poem

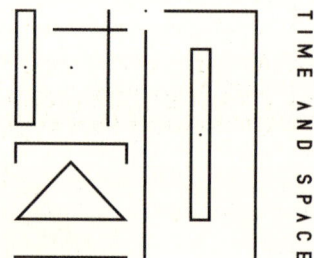

時間

TIME AND SPACE

THE LIFE OF THE SPIRIT MAY BE FAIRLY REPRESENTED IN DIAGRAM AS A LARGE ACUTE-ANGLED TRIANGLE DIVIDED HORIZONTALLY INTO UNEQUAL PARTS WITH THE NARROWEST SEGMENT UPPERMOST. THE LOWER THE SEGMENT THE GREATER IT IS IN BREADTH, DEPTH, AND AREA.
— WASSILY KANDINSKY

TRIANGLE

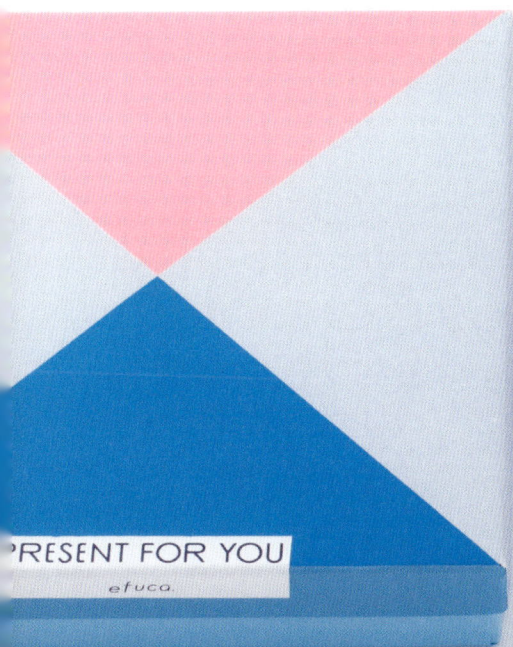

PRESENT FOR YOU

efuca.

PRESENT FOR YOU

efuca.

efuca.

efuca. is a candy store in Hyogo, Japan. Yuka Ito's sweets from efuca. are so colorful that the designer designs a package in a color palette that matches the sweets, hoping to enable the customers to feel the fun of the sweets from the package.

Designer Yuka Shiramoto | Studio SHIRO Inc. | Client efuca.

Geometry Now !

FB AIR Mural Commission

The designer was commissioned by the Facebook Artist in Residence Program to create a mural for the new Facebook offices in Ballbridge, Dublin, Ireland. In the mural, the designer played with variations on simple geometric patterns, drawing one line at the time. That mix of the geometric and the organic shapes, and the balance between the hand-drawn line and the exactness of shapes give it an energy of its own. Layering creates new color combinations and unexpected compositions of positive and negative shapes.

Designer Paul Bokslag | Client Facebook Artist in Residence Program

IT IS THE UNFORESEEABLE THAT CREATES THE EVENT. — GEORGES BRAQUE

UNFORESEEABLE

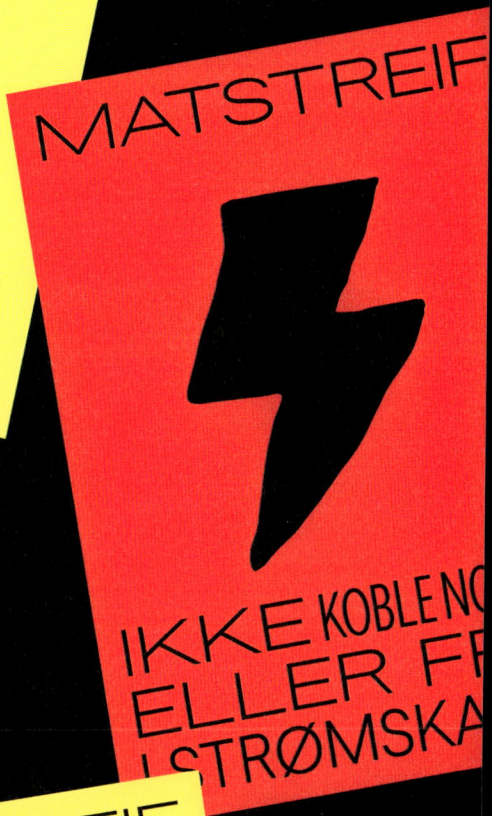

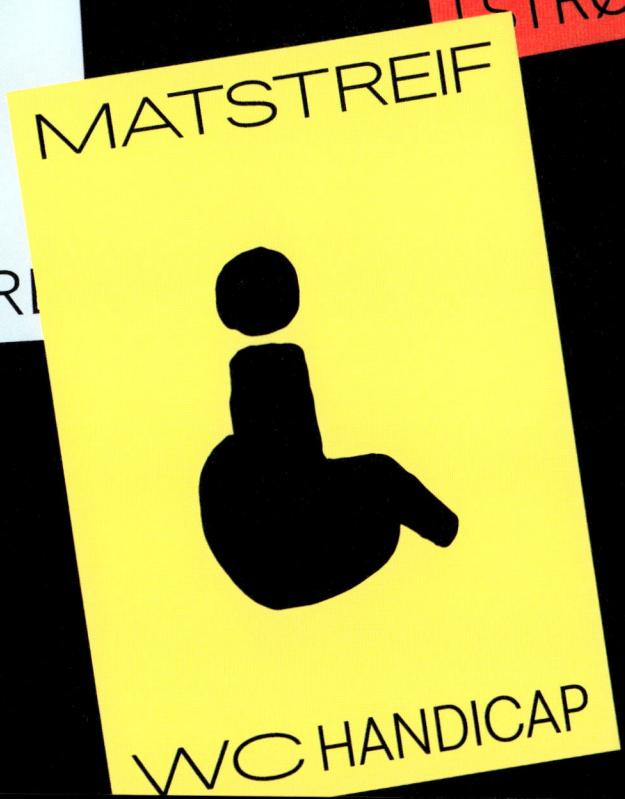

City Culture Institute

City Culture Institute creates events in the public space and supports cultural initiatives in Gdańsk, Poland. The essential motifs upon which its visual identity is developed are monochrome. The motifs are geometric compositions consisting of three quadrangles and a circle and filling the space to the edges. The design resembles shapes of maps, structures of a top-view city, which is filled with life by the Institute's initiatives. For the consistency of the design, the studio developed a script which generated them based on a few simple rules with randomness. All the printed materials was done with a 100% recycled paper.

Designer Marcin Gwiazdowski, Kama Schinwelska | Studio Elipsy |

Client City Culture Institute

instytut kultury miejskiej
TARG RAKOWY 11
INSTYTUT KULTURY MIEJSKIEJ
W KUNSZCIE WODNYM

WSPIERAMY
TWORZYMY

instytut kultury miejskiej
ZA SCENA
O TYM, JAK FESTIWALE WYGLĄDAJĄ ZZA SCENY
PIKNIK MIEJSKI
TARG RAKOWY 11
14 LIPCA
11 SIERPNIA
1 WRZEŚNIA
2018
AKADEMIA GDAŃSKA 2018
GDAŃSK – MIASTO, KTÓREGO NIE MA

instytut kultury miejskiej
MARZEC 2019

Geometry Now !

Instytut kultury miejskiej

MIASTA

MITY

MISTYFIKACJE

O TOPOSEMIOTYCE PRZESTRZENI MIEJSKICH

cykl wykładów
w Instytucie Kultury
Miejskiej w Gdańsku
2018/19

Matstreif

Matstreif is a food festival taking place in Oslo, Norway. The identity is filled with life, taste, humor and energy. It is in vibrant colors which inspired by the taste senses, featuring a distinct illustration style. The studio found inspiration in the established category language of food festivals. The farmers and their food were put in the center and became rock stars for the weekend. The studio designed a custom typeface, Smaks Sans, a variable type was kneaded out across all formats.

Designer Nicklas Haslestad, Vetle Majgren Uthaug | Studio Scandinavian Design Group | Client Innovation Norway

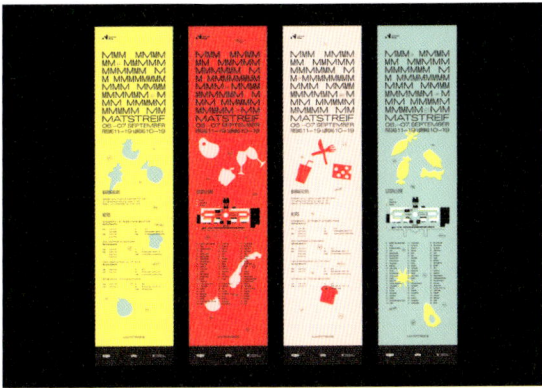

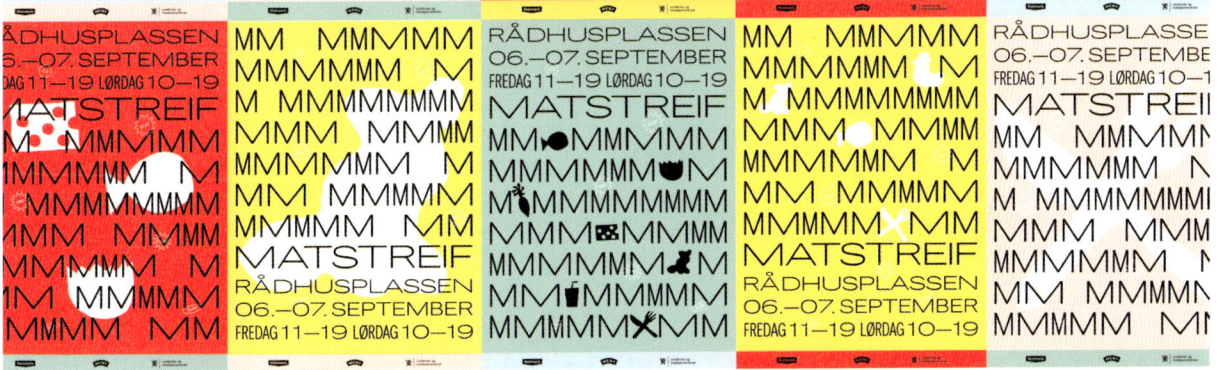

Geometry Now !

ØLMENY

MATSTREIF

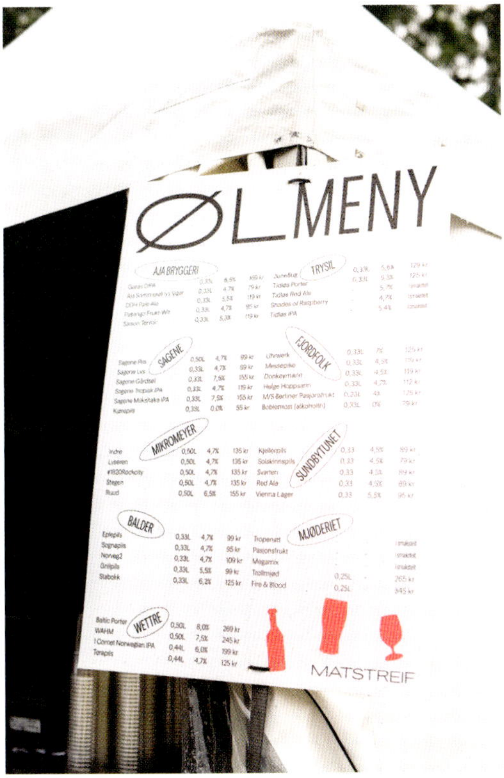

CREW

NOE PÅ TUNGA? SPYTT UT!

DO YOU THINK GEOMETRIC SHAPES ARE TIME-SENSITIVE IN GRAPHIC DESIGN? DO YOU THINK THEY WILL BE SUBJECT TO THE CHANGES IN THE AESTHETIC CULTURE?

Zubin Jhaveri

I think geometric shapes are timeless in design. It has been part of ancient architecture and many art movements. I think over the years what has changed is the extent of how much of geometry is used in design. In the present time whatever is considered futuristic is related to how geometry will be used and perceived. There was a time when sharp edges gave a futurist look. That gave way to smoothed edges and subtler look in design. The geometry is always there, just in a more indirect form.

Lung-Hao Chiang

Advancement of materials unavoidably influences how geometric shapes are being used in design. For example, different techniques, like laser engraving or printing, usually come with different limitations in presenting the design; pixels of electronic media always affect the design of geometric shapes. There is no absolute aesthetic culture, so designers should carefully evaluate the audience, the location and the purpose, presenting the design according to the situation.

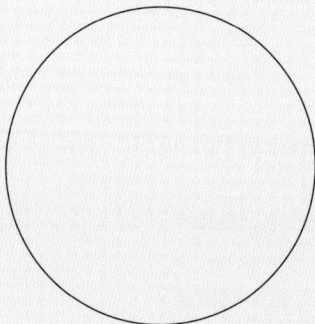

Xtian Miller

Certain aesthetic choices may avoid using geometric shapes, but overall I don't think they will ever go out of fashion. They're quite versatile and useful to so many forms of art and design, and can be leveraged in many different ways to fit different aesthetic preferences. Geometric form, especially sacred geometry, is inherent in nature but has also been used for thousands of years in both architecture and art. Saying a circle or square time-sensitive is like saying a particular color is time-sensitive. It's also worth pointing out that even the designs without any apparent geometric shapes contain some intentional or unintentional geometric considerations, whether it's in containers, spacing, or typographic form.

Yuka Shiramoto

I don't think geometric shapes are time-sensitive. I can't say that they're always free from influence by aesthetic culture, but I don't think it's going to have a big impact. Many geometric patterns exist in nature and have been familiar to humans for a long time. That's why I'm unconsciously familiar with it, so I think it's a design that's always familiar to me.

YOHAK DESIGN STUDIO

I think the simple forms of geometric shapes have always been used. They are an integral part of our lives. This is very apparent if we look back at ancient times: we can see them very clearly in ornaments from times when there were few tools, and complicated shapes were difficult to produce by hand. They're also the basic forms from which other shapes are derived, so I think they're limitless.

Chris Page

I don't think geometric shapes and patterns have a shelf life. Graphic designers have been using shapes as core elements in their designs for centuries from Herbert Bayer of the Bauhaus school to Hey Studio and Camille Walala's bold usage of shapes today. Each using a similar shape, pattern, or form but treated differently to align with cultural tastes.

Nick Barclay

They go in and out of fashion. But as they are so important to the fundamentals of design, they always come back into trend.

Ayaka Shimizu

I don't think the geometric shape itself is time-sensitive, but I think that the sense of the times influences layout, typefaces and colors around the geometric shape.

Totoro

I believe that geometry is now a trend in design. For example, many famous brands now have adjusted their logos to look like more geometric and flattening. As for whether it is time-sensitive, I think it is, but compared with other elements, geometric shapes are less likely to go out of style.

STUDIO NA.EO

No of course. Geometric shapes will never subject to changes of times, as, after all, graphic design is based on dots, lines and planes.

Gregory Page

In my opinion, they aren't time-sensitive. They are a worldwide norm and the graphic design scene and culture has a long relationship with geometric shapes, therefore it is logic for me that they will still be used by designers in the future.

out.o studio

I believe geometric shapes will never go out of style, but as time goes by, how these shapes are presented and how they are organized will changed. Historically, geometric shapes can be traced back to as early as the Neolithic Age when people used shapes to separate different tools. And when we were young, geometric shapes were also very important in helping us to be acquainted with the world. Abstract geometric shapes allows a very large space for the audience to imagine. With different life experiences, people will have different perceptions of the design, which might be what makes geometric shapes quite attractive.

Sakai Hiroko

I think geometric shapes are universally used in all ages. They are design elements that are not easily influenced by trends and times

Scandinavian Design Group

The beauty of geometric shapes is that they will, in my opinion, never go out of style. Geometry is timeless and designers always approach them in new ways, making it constantly interesting and engaging.

VARIATION DOES NOT MEAN EVOLUTION. IF AN ARTIST VARIES HIS MODE OF EXPRESSION THIS ONLY MEANS THAT HE HAS CHANGED HIS MANNER OF THINKING, AND IN CHANGING, IT MIGHT BE FOR THE BETTER OR IT MIGHT BE FOR THE WORSE.
— PABLO PICASSO

VARIATION

2020 Visions

2020 Visions by Matt W. Moore of MWM Graphics is an exploration of classic icons and symbols. Multiple versions of each were inspired by the original themes and/or concepts of the classic icons.

Designer Matt W. Moore | Studio MWM Graphics

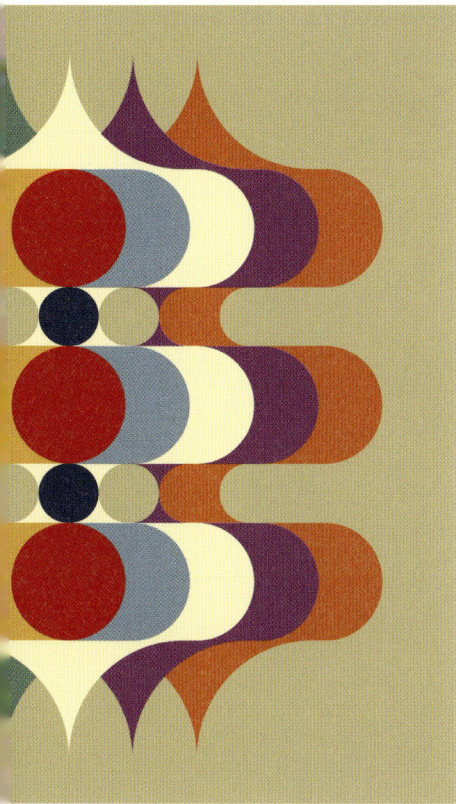

Taraf

The goal of this project was to create a package design for a non-existing brand called Taraf, an Arabic word that means luxury. It is a premium chocolate brand that specializes in offering Arabic chocolates. The brand offers three traditional Arabic flavors, such as chocolate with dates, rosewater, and almond. Besides, arabesque art and architecture inspired the design of the package.

Designer Nora Alzaidi

TARAF
ARABIC CHOCOLATE

CHOCOLATE
WITH DATES

70g / 2.5 oz

TARAF
ARABIC CHOCOLATE

CHOCOLATE
WITH ROSEWATER

70g / 2.5 oz

TARAF
ARABIC CHOCOLATE

CHOCOLATE
WITH ALMOND

70g / 2.5 oz

MindTalk Posters

"Create brand new looks", meaning to employ new ways of thinking and communicating when presenting normal things, is the very inspiration behind the design of the poster. The designer chose a series of simple shapes as the basis of the design, and turned them into a rather special visual language with special adjustments.

Designer Liang Zhuosi | Studio TOPYS

甲策展的

思维

创造全新

商业体验

Vol.26

mind
talk
创意公开课

温昊 Billy Wen & 杨源丰 Yeoh Guan Hong
上海 SuperNatureDesign 联合创始人
数字艺术创造商业体验价值

傅熙林 Celine
北京 2x4 北京工作室合伙人兼创意总监
品牌策展实现市场沟通

时间
7月13日 14:30-17:30

地点
科兴科学园国际会议中心

扫码
了解更多

Kigi (キギ) was invited to be the guest giving the keynote speech to MindTalk. Kigi means trees in Japanese, so in the poster design, the designer aimed at visualizing the idea of Kigi (trees) growing into a forest.

Designer Liang Zhuosi | Studio TOPYS

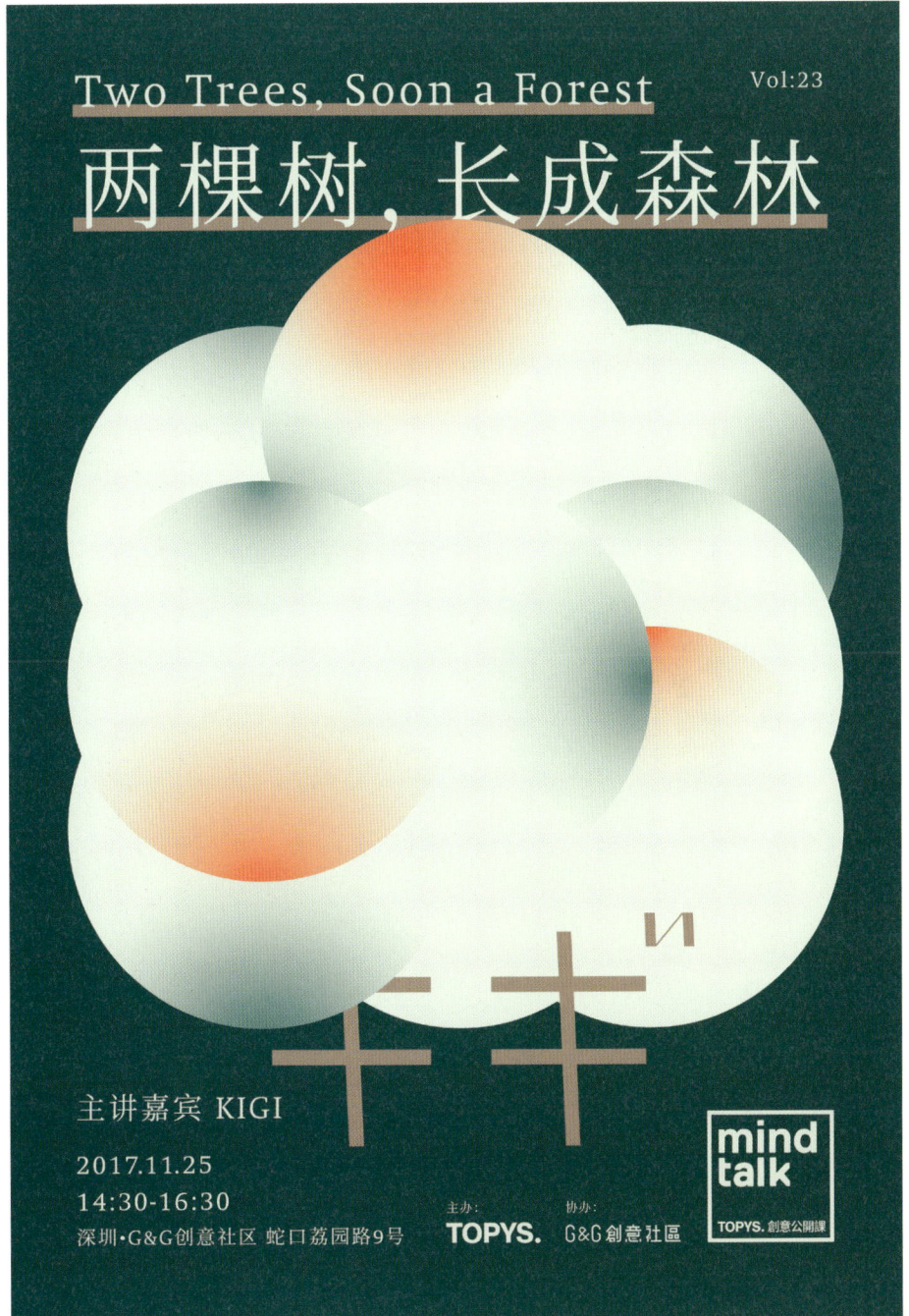

JL design, a studio established by Johnason Lo, is good at telling stories of brands with the use of Motion Graphic. Each frame of the motion is quite unique. When putting together, these frames help to deliver a complete story. The designer, thus, ingeniously played with the buttons symbol, including button of "play", "pause" and "fast-forward", and put them into different geometric shapes to represent Motion Graphic.

Designer Wang Haishan | Studio TOPYS

"Yeasts in Metropolis" is a program aiming at advancing design in the urban area. Whether it is renewal of signboards or box substations, the program focuses on the participation of creative individuals, namely those who are in the city, constantly contributing to the urban renewal, and as the designer believe, all these individuals are the Yeasts in Metropolis.

Designer Wang Haishan | Studio TOPYS

IF I PAINT A WILD HORSE, YOU MIGHT NOT SEE THE HORSE... BUT SURELY YOU WILL SEE THE WILDNESS! — PABLO PICASSO

WILDNESS

Caracol Bar

Sometimes Always was asked to design the brand identity for Caracol Bar, a listening bar with different DJs playing every day. Starting from sketching, the studio first took the basic form of Caracol (snail in portuguese) and reduced it to the minimum, a circle. Then, the studio created 4 different types of circles in a palette of 9 different colors. Finally, 7 different possibilities of layout was created.

Studio Sometimes Always | Client Caracol Bar

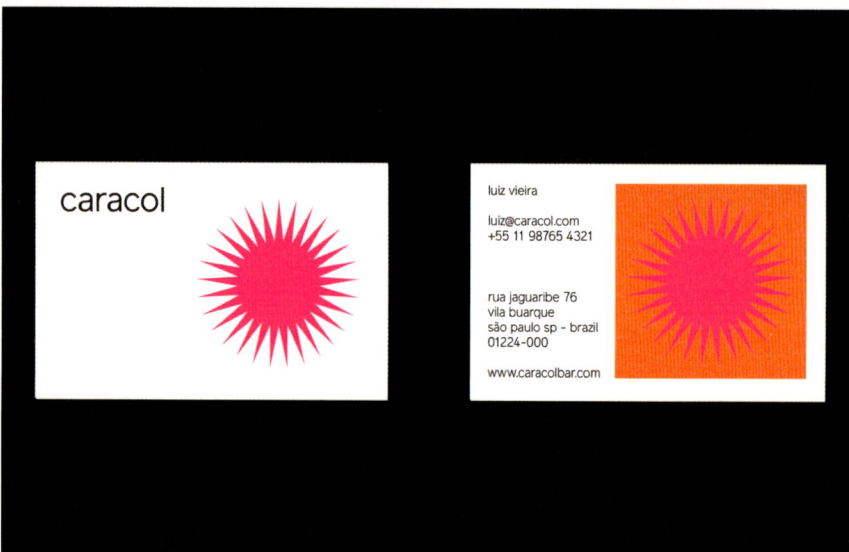

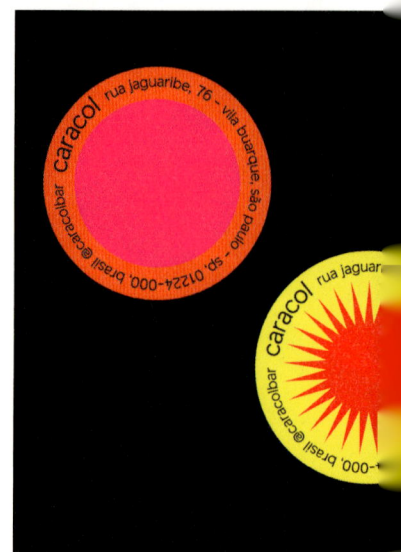

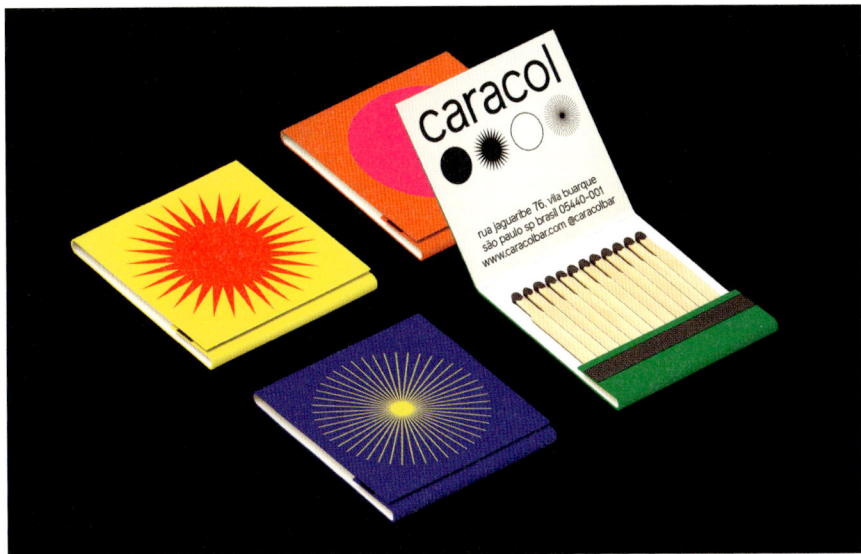

ON&ON,
BLACKJACK —
WILASCO

This is a visual identity project for digital single release. The song talks about the difficulty of leaving behind the adventures that a night can bring — taking sips and sips more, watching hours and hours go by and trying to get home before dawn "on & on", something that many of us know how it is. The challenge was to communicate this on the cover and in the communication pieces, along with the atmosphere that the music brings.

Designer Raphael de Luca | Client WILASCO

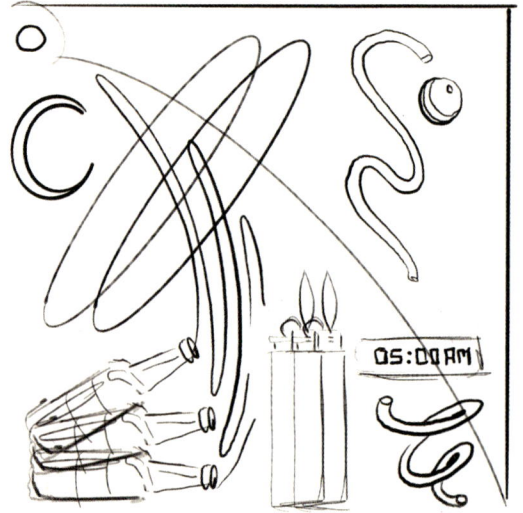

Geometry Now !

WE DOCUMENT, EXPLAIN, JUSTIFY, CONSTRUCT AND ORGANIZE: THESE ARE GOOD THINGS, BUT WE DO NOT SUCCEED IN COMING TO THE WHOLE. BUT WE MAY AS WELL CALM DOWN: CONSTRUCTION IS NOT ABSOLUTE. OUR VIRTUE IS THIS: BY CULTIVATING THE EXACT WE HAVE LAID THE FOUNDATIONS FOR A SCIENCE OF ART, INCLUDING THE UNKNOWN X.
— PAUL KLEE

X — THE UNKNOWN

MORTO UN PAPA 😞

Gallina vecchia

AL

SE SON ROSE 😊

SI STAVA MEGLIO 😞

è pan bagnato

SUL

Mezzodetto

Old sayings are the symbol of the cultural heritage of the past, witnessing the development of the history, social norms, judgments and advices. What is the popular truth nowadays? Mezzodetto is a project that aims to highlight the vulnerability of popular wisdom, leaving the formulation of new truths to chance. Turn the wheel, and a new reality is coming.

Designer Ballarini Lorenzo, Caricasole Elena, Ricciarini Andrea | Studio MEZZOPIENO STUDIO

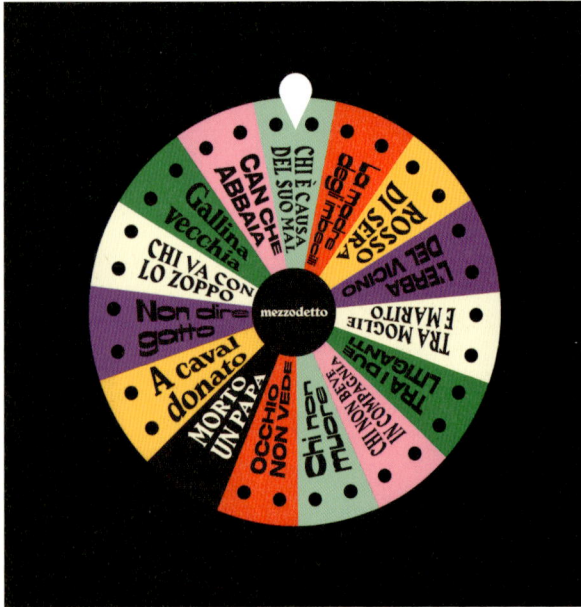

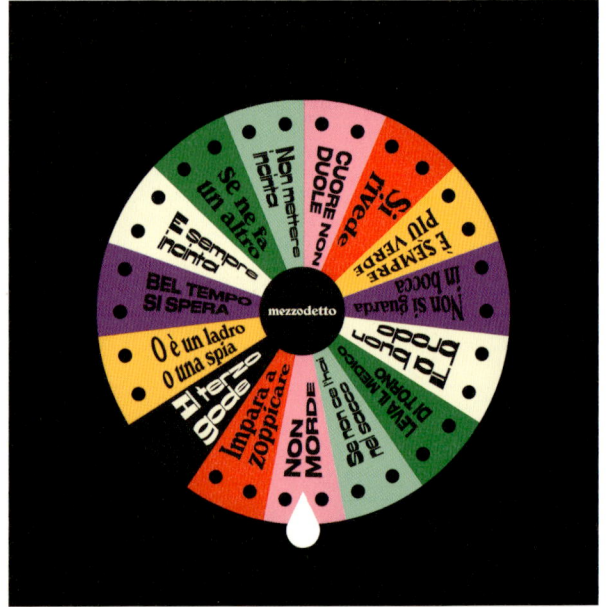

CHI È CAUSA DEL SUO MAL è sempre incinta

CHI NON BEVE IN COMPAGNIA impara a zoppicare

CHI VA CON LO ZOPPO NON MORDE

Gallina vecchia MEZZA BELLEZZA

Chi non muore LEVA IL MEDICO DI TORNO

SE SON ROSE è pan bagnato

ROSSO DI SERA Si rivede

SI STAVA MEGLIO SUL LATTE VERSATO

TRA MOGLIE E MARITO il terzo gode

Branding & Identity for Pepita de Oliva Studio

Pepita de Oliva Studio is an independent studio offering customized furniture service, and a vintage shop characterized by its reassuring and relaxing atmosphere. It is a perfect place to lose a couple of hours in the midst of wonderful design and art pieces. The designer decided to go with something that recalls a modular space in constant motion, as the place is one of the most important architecture studios in the city. The logo is a motional one, which is highly recognizable even if it keeps changing.

Designer Marco Oggian | Client Pepita de Oliva Studio

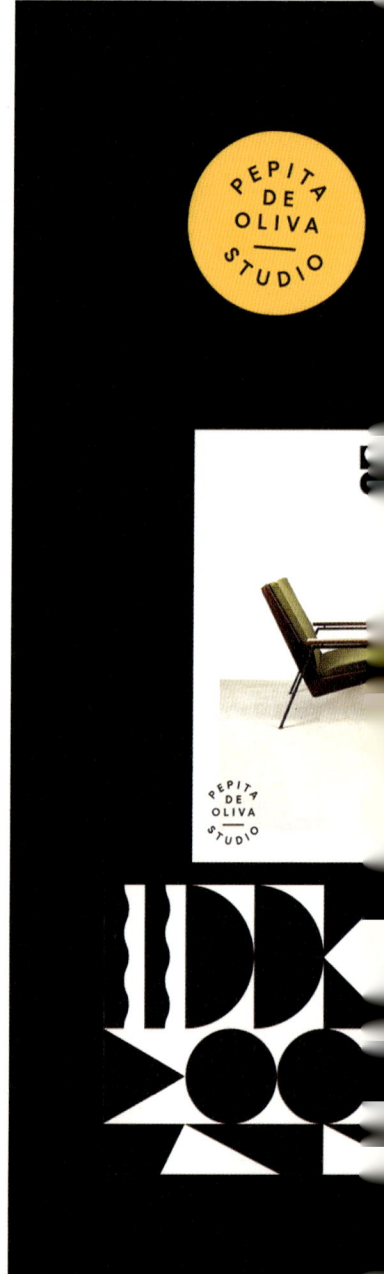

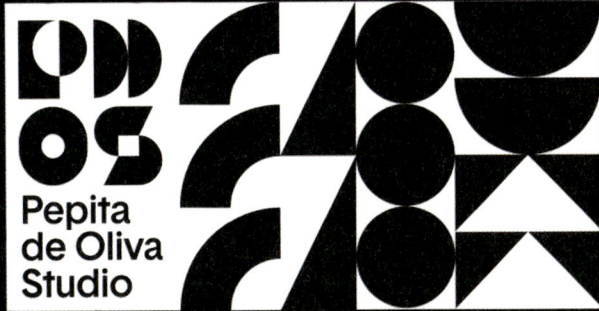

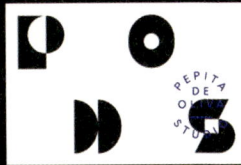

One Hundred Stories, One Face

The idea behind '100' was to represent one hundred different iconic people with the same base, namely the same eyes and the same mouth. The designer treated the elements with simple geometric figures, making them recognizable only through the details and the colors which render them unique. The project allows us to understand how our experience, age and education lead us to recognize one figure over another, and above all, it forces us to realize how the small details make everyone unique.

Designer Marco Oggian | Client Pocko Face App

Designer Marco Oggian | Client A Coruña city hall

Eastpak Campaign

Whether it is a single illustration or an entire campaign project, simple geometric shapes and 5 bright colors palette is more than enough to compose the designer's world.

Designer Marco Oggian | Client Eastpak worldwide

FRIENDS
AND
FAMILY

INCOMING
CALL

MARCO OGGIAN

TO BE YOUNG, REALLY YOUNG, TAKES A VERY LONG TIME.
— PABLO PICASSO

YOUNG

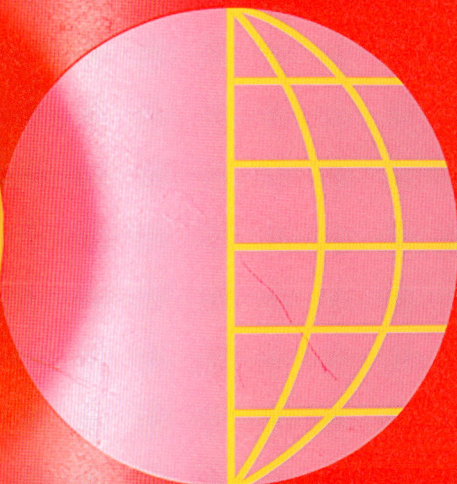

RAD Branding

"RAD" stands for "Random Absorbed Dose of Fruits". Rad is all you ever dreamed: It's a sparkling tea, organic and unsweetened. Surprisingly, it has the most unexpected combinations of fruits delivered in a can. Bold and eccentric color combos are mixed with a 1970s vibe to give a surreal mood. Having fun with retro slang terms to bring a more sassy and daring brand tone.

Designer Luján Borzi, Pia Alive, Florencia Tasso, Milton Gonzalez, Valeria Moreiro |
Studio NOT REAL | Client NOT REAL CREATIVE S.L.

RAD*

Lime & Watermelon • Papaya & Blueberry • Coconut & Strawberry
Banana & Peppermint • Grapefruit & Pomegranate

RAD*
Random Absorbed
Dose of Fruits
Unsweetened
& Organic

New flavours
for you!

Unsweetened
& Organic

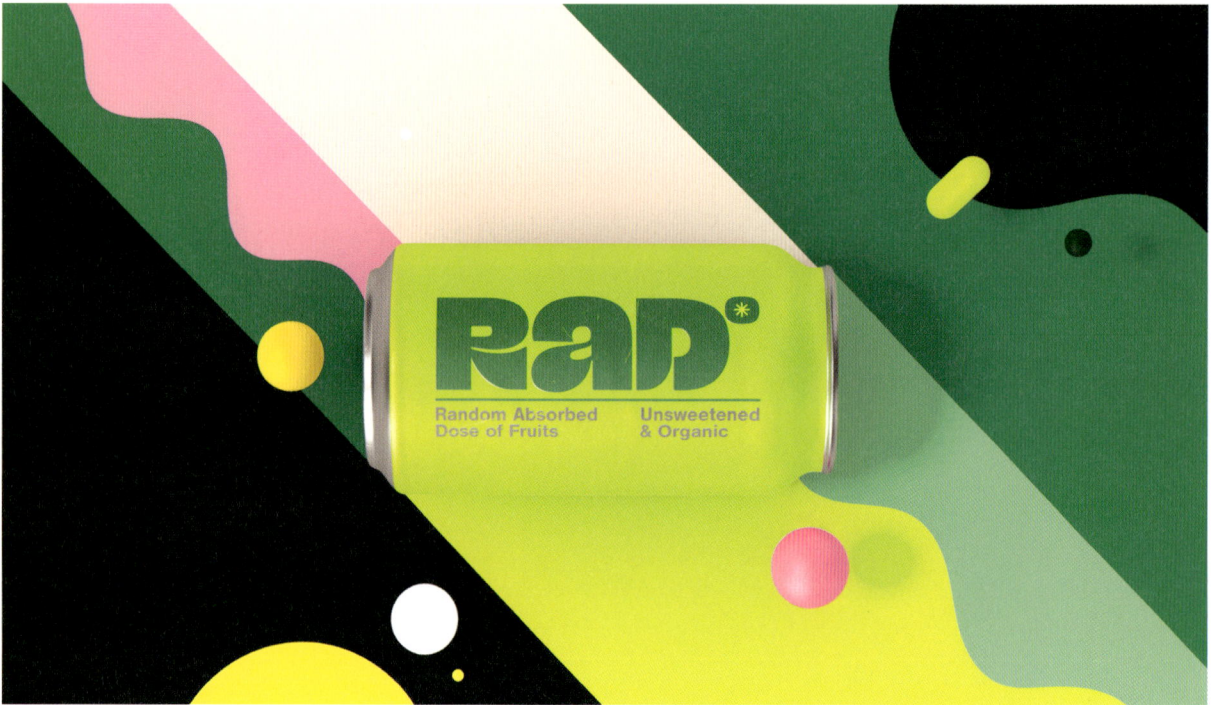

Geometry Now !

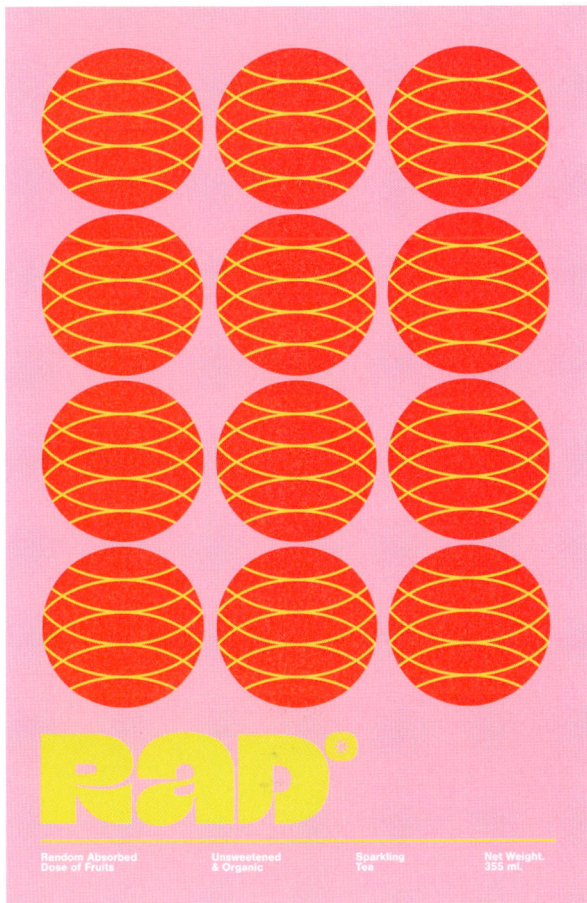

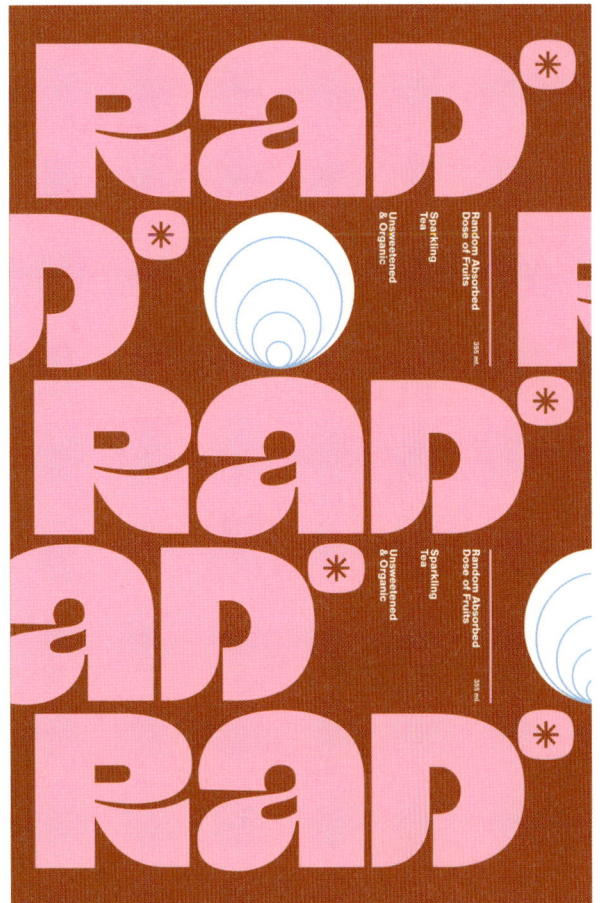

Banbou Moon Cake

No single peaceful night in childhood goes by without mother humming "Twinkle twinkle little star..." at the bedside. Mid-autumn Day is a day of reunion, and also a day for us to savor memories of our beloved ones. The designer put his feelings into the design, incorporating the stars into the beautifully organized blue and white background. The delicately designed stars in the package shine like diamonds, whispering how much the designer misses his mother.

Designer Yu Ziyi, Lin Nan, Quan Kangtian | Studio Y.STUDIO | Client BANBOU PATISSERIE & COFFEE

WHAT MIGHT BE TAKEN FOR A PRECOCIOUS GENIUS IS THE GENIUS OF CHILDHOOD. WHEN THE CHILD GROWS UP, IT DISAPPEARS WITHOUT A TRACE. IT MAY HAPPEN THAT THIS BOY WILL BECOME A REAL PAINTER SOMEDAY, OR EVEN A GREAT PAINTER. BUT THEN HE WILL HAVE TO BEGIN EVERYTHING AGAIN, FROM ZERO.
— PABLO PICASSO

ZERO

KANSEIDO

KANSEIDO

KANSEIDO is a candy store in Shizuoka, Japan, selling both Japanese and Western sweets. The designer who was asked to handle the logo and package renewal tended to make it fit well with people of all ages by using delicately designed combination of geometric shapes. Trying to express the fun of eating sweets, the designer employed a colorful color scheme.

Designer Yuka Shiramoto | Studio SHIRO Inc. | Client KANSEIDO

Poster for
Otl Aicher
Exhibition

Otl Aicher (1922–1991) is a graphic designer, typographer, and professor of architecture and design at the Ulm School of Design, which he co-founded with Max Bill, and Inge Aicher-Scholl. The studio was invited to design two A2 posters for an exhibition commemorating this brilliant and admirable designer we will always look up to.

Studio empatía

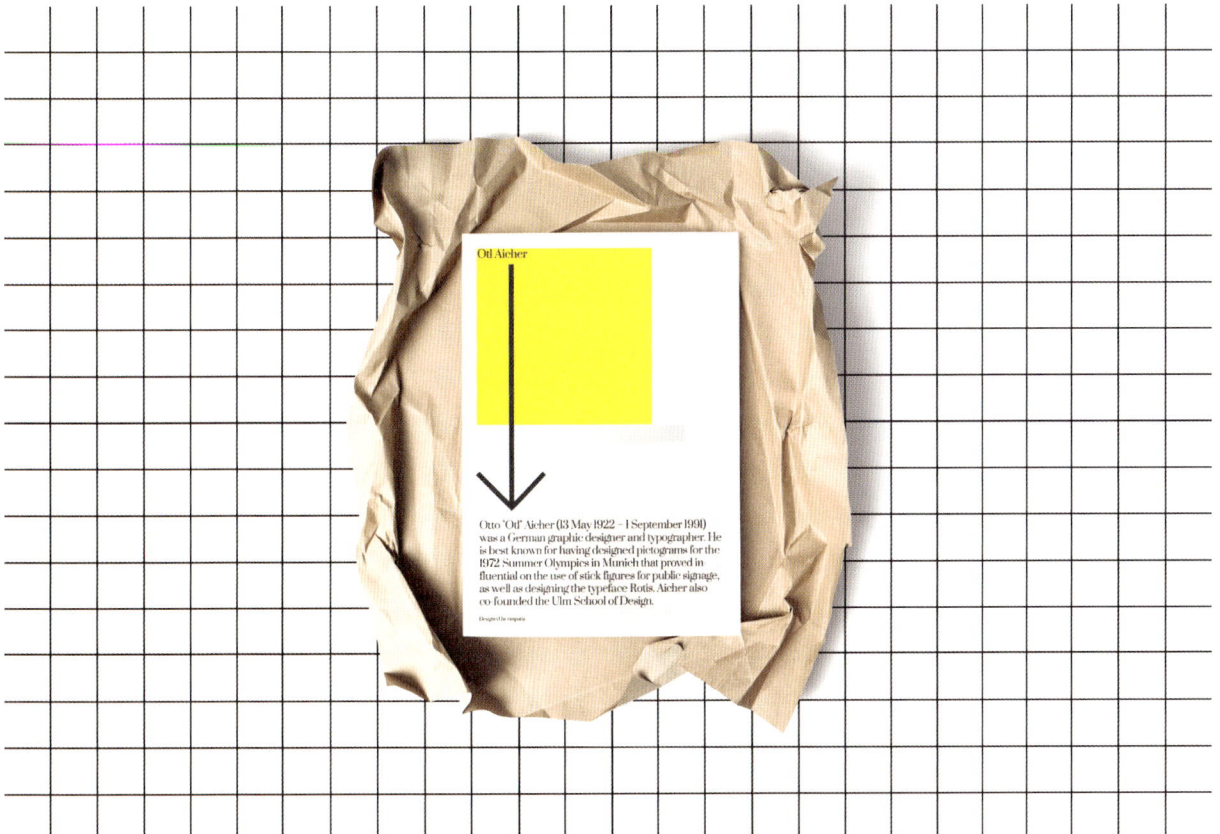

SPEAKING OF GEOMETRIC SHAPES IN DESIGN, WHICH ARTIST OR WHICH GENRE, SCHOOL OR MOVEMENT WOULD COME TO YOUR MIND? WHY?

Johanne Lian Olsen

Geometry has always been used in design and some, like Bauhaus, are more known for basing their aesthetics on geometry. Personally I find it more interesting to look at artists for inspiration, and the artworks of Ellsworth Kelly are a favorite of mine. The simplicity, combinations of shapes and shapes versus space are really intriguing. Another is John Baldessari with his play with overlapping geometric shapes on photography/printing. The play between simplicity and details, "organic" and "geometric" is inspiring.

Götz Gramlich

Basic geometrical forms, whether they are large or small, define the face of nature. And in our human nature, striving to imitate nature is deeply anchored. So it is not surprising that these forms have been with us since the beginning of mankind. Therefore, all cultures and artists did and will deal with them again and again. I personally appreciate the approach of the Bauhaus, maybe because I was invited as a guest professorship at the Bauhaus in Weimar, or because their visual language was similarly radically reduced as their basic forms.

YOHAK DESIGN STUDIO

Japanese family crests came to my mind, although I don't have any particular attachment to them. There are very few occasions when family crests are used in modern Japan, but I have lots of chances to see them because they've become integrated into forms of culture that are close to me personally — old books, movies, comics, local festivals, and so on.

STUDIO NA.EO

De Stijl certainly is remarkable. And I personally like Bruno Munari, one of the futuristic artists, who involved in varied visual arts, including graphic design. I have seen toys and books he made for kids. They are very special in color combination and geometric structure.

Ayaka Shimizu

Probably most designers are the same, but I will particularly think of Bauhaus. I think it is a remarkable school that explored geometric shapes not only in graphic design, but also in many other fields related to design.

Makebardo

The first that comes to our mind is the Bauhaus because we feel inspired by it and we take it as a reference in our design. Without a doubt, its legacy in using geometry in different disciplines was revolutionary. Its minimalism and rationalism still influence the contemporary design. On the other hand, we cannot leave out Pre-Columbian cultures and their immense beauty when it comes to geometric use. More near in history, we could name Ellsworth Kelly or Yayoi Kusama, but naming someone is always unfair because one is made up of many references and all are valuable.

Chris Page

The Memphis Group has to be one of my favorites for their use of energetic colors and contrasting geometric patterns. I love how the shapes originally designed for printing influenced the furniture design, helping to form striking and crazy looking pieces.

Yuka Shiramoto

The first thing that came to my mind was Frank Lloyd Wright's design. He is my favorite architect. I especially like his stained glass design. His designs are novel, either symmetrical or asymmetrical. His geometric patterns are inspired by shapes in nature, so you can feel the warmth somewhere in his design.

Xtian Miller

For me personally, it's Swiss graphic design greats like Armin Hofmann and Josef Müller-Brockmann, who relied on the fundamental elements of graphic form to convey both simplicity and complexity, representation and abstraction. Through their unorthodox methodologies at the time, they pioneered the Swiss style and showed how point, line, and shape could allow designers to break away from illustration or photography and still make impactful work. There are obviously many other artists and designers throughout history who have used geometry and shapes to their advantage, but these guys in particular popularized a movement that had a huge impact on the industry.

Nick Barclay

If you're thinking of shapes I think your first stop will always be the Bauhaus, as they pretty much influenced all aspects of design by using them.

Gregory Page

Bauhaus, Piet Mondrian, Max Bill and Max Miedinger, just to name a few!

Monika Olbrycht

For me it's definitely art deco style, because I believe it changed the way of thinking about geometry. Geometry, which usually comes to mind as simple, is becoming more and more sophisticated and so are the shapes that the artists are using. In this style, geometry is related with nature, something that is normally opposite to it. I think this is what makes geometry really interesting for me and this is now showing new ways to think about geometry in a creative, fun way.

Ke Pengmin

I would think of Bauhaus and the Modern Movement. Also I would think of Paul Klee, an expressionist painter who is fond of using lines and geometric blocks of colors massively. His works, abstract and filled with symbolizing visual language, are like drawings of kids. But I only know little about painting, and Paul Klee just come to my mind. Few years ago, Kasai Kaoru redesigned the book, *Paul Klee Tagebücher 1989 — 1918,* in JAGDA Award 2019. Chinese artists Xiaomage & Chengzi also redesigned one of Paul Klee's book.

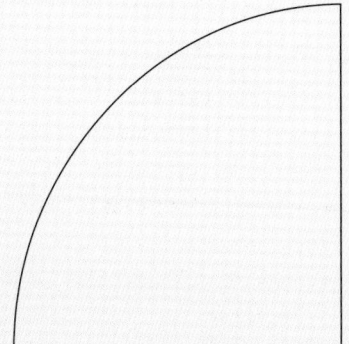

INDEX

GEOMETRY NOW! DESIGNING FOR TOMORROW

©2021 Sendpoints Publishing Co., Ltd.

First printing of the first edition, September 2021

sendp●ints

EDITED & PUBLISHED BY Sendpoints Publishing Co., Ltd.
PUBLISHER: Lin Gengli
PUBLISHING DIRECTOR: Nicole Lo
CHIEF EDITOR: Nicole Lo
EXECUTIVE EDITOR: Huang Baomin
DESIGN DIRECTOR: Wu Dongyan
EXECUTIVE ART EDITOR: Chen Anying
TRANSLATOR: Xu Chao
PROOFREADER: Huang Chujun
ILLUSTRATOR: 小野 itoe

REGISTERED ADDRESS: Room 15A Block 9 Tsui Chuk Garden, Wong Tai Sin, Kowloon, Hong Kong, China
TEL: +852-35832323 / **FAX:** +852-35832448
OFFICE ADDRESS: 7F, No.9-1 Anning Street, Jinshazhou Road, Baiyun District, Guangzhou, China
TEL: +86-20-89095121 / **FAX:** +86-20-89095206
BEIJING OFFICE: Room 513, 5th Floor, Building 1, Longde Zijinjia, No.186 Litang Road, Changping District, Beijing, China
TEL: +86-10-84139071 / **FAX:** +86-10-84139071
SHANGHAI OFFICE: Room 302, Floor 3, Ningbo Road No.349, Huangpu District, Shanghai, China
TEL: +86-21-63523469 / **FAX:** +86-21-63523469

SALES TEAM: Philip Tsang
TEL: +86-20-81007895
EMAIL: sales@sendpoints.cn
WEBSITE: www.sendpoints.cn / www.spbooks.cn

ISBN 978-988-74767-7-1

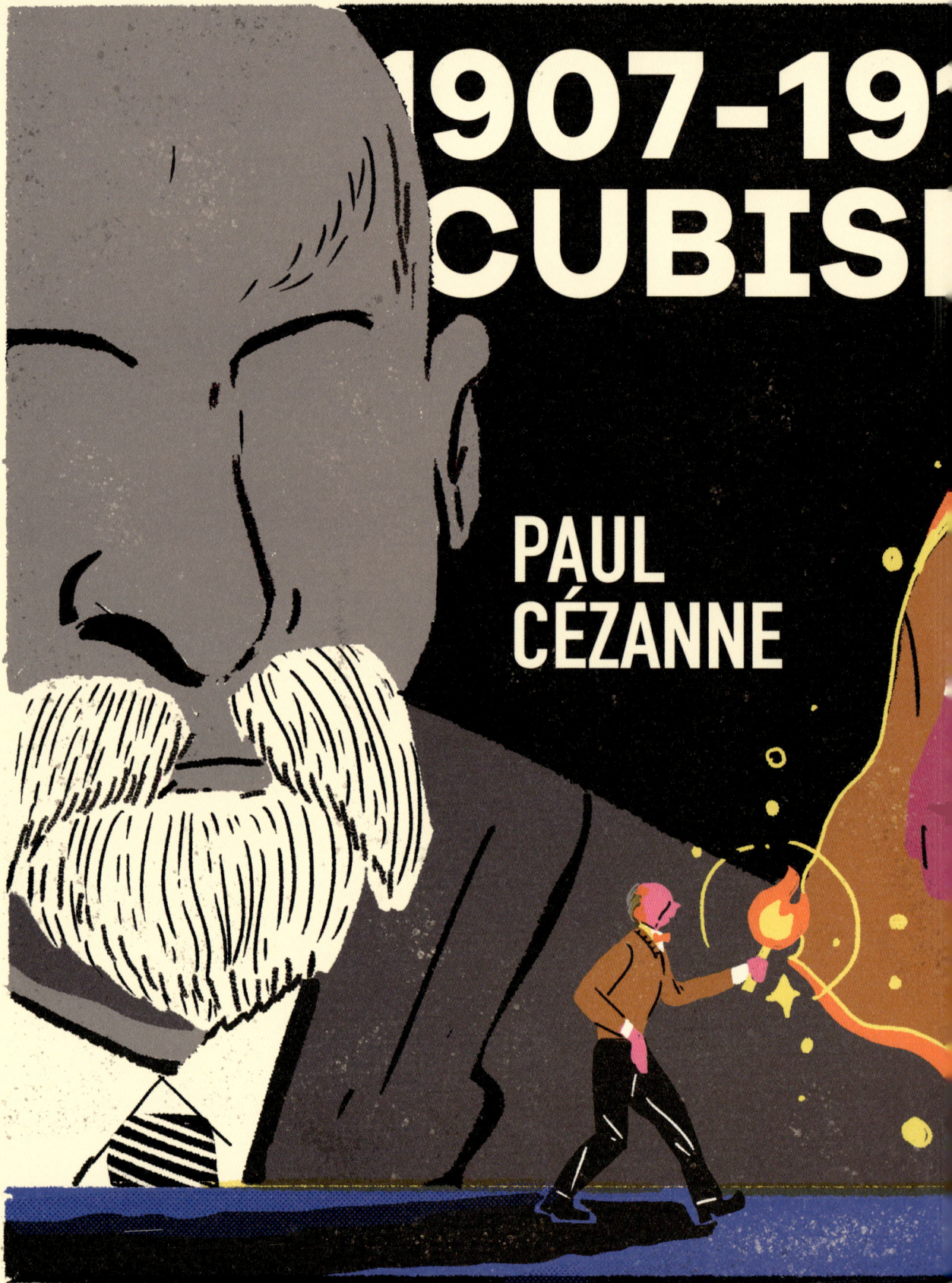

1907-19[...]
CUBISI[...]

PAUL
CÉZANNE